THE PARANOID PROPHET

THE PARANOID PROPHET

WILLIAM BACKUS

BETHANY HOUSE PUBLISHERS
MINNEAPOLIS, MINNESOTA 55438
A Division of Bethany Fellowship, Inc.

Published by Bethany House Publishers
A Division of Bethany Fellowship, Inc.
6820 Auto Club Road, Minneapolis, Minnesota 55438

Printed in the United States of America

Library of Congress Cataloging-in-Publication Data

Backus, William D.
    The paranoid prophet.

    1. Bible. O.T. Jonah—Psychology.
2. Jonah (Biblical prophet)   I. Title.
BS1605.5.B32   1986   224'.9206   86-11719
ISBN 0-87123-874-8

To Mebs

WILLIAM BACKUS, Ph.D., a psychologist and an ordained Lutheran clergyman, is Founder and Director of the Center for Christian Psychological Services in St. Paul, Minnesota. He has four grown children and he and his wife make their home in Forest Lake, Minnesota. He is an associate pastor of a large Lutheran congregation.

Table of Contents

Introduction 9
1. White Blotches 13
2. Nineveh University 23
3. Whither Shall I Flee from Thy Presence? 39
4. Shem 49
5. Away from the Presence 59
6. The Jonah Committee 67
7. Nachar on Love 73
8. Right Is Right and Wrong Is Wrong 81
9. Back to His God 89
10. Changes 97
11. Celebration 103
12. I Cannot Tell What This Love May Be
    Which Cometh to All But Not to Me 109
13. I Gave My Back to the Smiters 117

Introduction

There are some books in the Bible better taught by a psychologist than a theologian. Such a book is Jonah. To their discredit, some Christian teachers, writers, students, and theologians have wasted inordinate amounts of time on the fish swallowing the man and questions about the book's unity, and have paid precious little attention to the man who was swallowed.

What has fascinated me is Jonah's behavior. More gripping than the book's treatment of the gastrointestinal peculiarities of fish is the psychological peculiarity of its central character. What sort of personality would become involved with a jealous God like Yahweh, identify himself as a prophet of that God, and then stubbornly turn his back on what he knew to be God's pathway for him?

Jonah was no wimp. His revolt was open, direct and without apology. During the great discussion about anger between Yahweh and Jonah in the last chapter, the prophet very nearly defied God to His face. Risky behavior, to say the least, though Yahweh showed incredible patience and gentleness with His hard-headed prophet.

Jonah, of course, was a Hebrew who lived around 740 B.C. Bear in mind that centuries later, Jesus made Jonah's story a sign to the people of His generation. He specifically related Jonah's experience with the great fish in prophesying about His own death, burial and resurrection. (Unless you keep this parallel in mind, you will be unduly puzzled by the narrator's dreams and the hymn stanzas heading each chapter in this book.)

Had he lived in our time and culture, Jonah could surely have been a clinical case. It appears to me that, had he presented himself for clinical treatment in this day and age, he would have been given this diagnosis: Paranoid Personality Disorder.

The Psychologist as Storyteller

To come to terms with Jonah and his "diagnosis," I have chosen to tell the story out of the mouth of Jonah's imaginary psychotherapist, a God-fearing psychologist in Nineveh at the time of the prophet's visit to that city.

Though not a Hebrew, this psychologist has come to believe in the God of the Hebrews, and therefore was Jonah's choice for psychological help. Readers must not be so literal-minded as to point out that the science of psychology was unknown in Jonah's time, or they will have insurmountable difficulty with this entire book.

Some readers may be psychotherapists or counselors, and they will already know from experience how it feels to begin with a new client like Jonah. Others may only have supposed what that counselor-client relationship is like, imagining the rewards of bringing comfort to poor downhearted souls, grateful for your every wise word. What would-be counselor ever envisions getting involved with a client like Jonah? With patients like him, a therapist feels shut in with a room full of hostility, seething anger and unbounded suspicions. You find yourself on the defensive, feeling accused and guilty of negative sentiments the client suspects you harbor. Often, you feel you are trapped in a "no win" situation.

Given all those dynamics, I suspect it will be difficult for some to feel empathy for Jonah. Like any professional counselor, you must constantly remind yourself that this man is anguished by a sensitivity and grief so exquisite he must hide it under a cloak of wrath.

Revealing Jonah and the Ways of God

So my primary objective in this book is to reveal Jonah as I have come to understand him.

My second purpose is similar to that of the biblical book of Jonah: to reveal some of the ways of God. Since at least the days of the heretic Marcion, loose theology about the God of the Old Testament (of which there appears to be a superabundance these days) presents him as an irrascible, easily provoked dictator who seizes eagerly upon every excuse to lash out at somebody—anybody at all.

On the contrary: The book of Jonah presents no rigid deity just waiting to "get" people, but a God who, in contrast with His prophet, is infinitely loving, supremely patient and concerned for the smallest and most alienated of His creatures.

From my studies of Jonah, I have discovered something extraordinary about the God who works in human lives, and how He intervenes in nature to accomplish His plans with individuals and nations.

So What Kind of Book Are You Reading?

What kind of literature is this book about Jonah? It is not a book of history, since there is no effort to remain faithful to a historical period, nor is it, like my previous books, a didactic presentation on Christian psychology. Rather, I have taken the freedom to inject twentieth-century A.D. notions into a nominally eighth-century B.C. setting. I must note, too, that no character is meant to be a thinly veiled representation of any twentieth-century person, living or dead, although the *ideas* of some living persons are unabashedly represented and critiqued.

So what sort of book is *The Paranoid Prophet*? A novel? Perhaps. Fantasy? Maybe. Story theology? Possibly. Some early readers have suggested the book is more like a play or a long dialogue. I suggest you take this book on its own terms, as a story that weaves theology and psychology with philosophy. Its purpose is to help the reader grow in understanding and behavior pertinent to a walk of faith in Jesus Christ, the God with whom Jonah became angry enough to die.

William Backus
Forest Lake, Minnesota
March 1, 1986

1

White Blotches

He whose path no records tell
Hath descended into hell;
He the strong man armed hath bound
And in highest heav'n is crowned. Hallelujah!**

It was one of those days every therapist dreads: The day of the full moon. Maybe that had something to do with the utterly improbable stories and claims my clients had been presenting. One woman was convinced that the god Bel had revealed that her husband was about to murder her; a man became furious with me because I refused to intervene in a dispute he was having with his employer; and there were more similarly distraught seekers after wholeness.

Mercifully, the day was nearly over. My last patient was to be a new client named Jonah.

Wearily, I closed my eyes and tried to recall the somewhat distressing conversation I'd had two days before with my best friend, Shem, about this man Jonah. What was it Shem had said? I envisioned the look of surprise on Shem's face when, as he stood here gazing out of my office window, I casually mentioned that Jonah was seeking my help. His jaw slacked with amazement, Shem wheeled around.

"You have an appointment with the prophet, Jonah?" he asked, incredulous.

---

*Christus ist erstanden, Michael Weisse, 1531; tr. Catherine Winkworth, 1863.

"I'd heard he was looking for a therapist. Do you have *any* idea what this man has accomplished in Nineveh?"

My face had warmed a little with embarrassment: Shem, although he lived in Babylon, always heard the local gossip before I did. His academic contacts at nearby Nineveh University kept him well informed, while I, as a busy clinician, spent most of my time listening to the troubles of my patients.

"No," I replied, tilting my chair back so as to maintain my casual air, "I never heard of Jonah until he sent a messenger to arrange an appointment." I realized as I said it that Shem must be thinking I kept my head buried in the sand, and I was beginning to wish I hadn't mentioned the upcoming appointment. I had only thought that Shem, a Hebrew himself, might be interested.

He was more than interested. He was excited. He came away from the window and paced the floor in front of me, gesturing excitedly as he spoke. "Jonah has turned this city upside down! He arrived in Nineveh out of nowhere, proclaiming imminent doom for the city if people did not 'repent.' The marvel is that people *listened*. Even people in high places—the emperor himself, professors at the university, traders, and all sorts of people you would expect to have laughed Jonah off as a crackpot. But this beats all—now he's coming to see a psychologist! Well, wha'daya know?" he finished with a whistle.

The scene faded, and I opened my eyes again. Now it was time to see Jonah. As I rose from my chair in the consulting room, I couldn't help wondering what this extraordinary man could possibly want from me. With his registration form in hand, I walked into the waiting room to find him. The moment I laid eyes on the huge stranger, I felt we were in for a tough session. "Mr. Jonah?"

His rough, homespun clothes and the greeting he grunted at me as he rose from his chair told me he was from the country—the backwoods of the empire, more likely. And, as

I turned to lead him back into the consulting room, I noticed his skin: covered with white, flaky blotches!

When I closed the door to the consulting room behind us, I motioned for him to take a comfortable cushioned seat opposite my desk. As I picked up my notepad and pencil and seated myself, I noticed that Jonah had chosen a straight-backed chair instead—moreover, he perched himself at the front edge of the seat as if to keep himself ready for a hasty exit. I tried to relax at the desk and, for the first time, carefully observe this man.

My first impression was of *more* white blotches. They covered his face, arms and hands. What had caused them? I had never seen the like. Behind the blotches was sunburn, from the bald patch on top of his head down to the massive calves showing beneath his long tunic. But more than his badly abused skin, I noticed at once what counselors call "the paranoid headlights"—the bulging eyes, open so wide that the whites show all around the pupils. Jonah's eyes darted about the office, noting every item: the sofa, bookshelves, lamps, tables; every corner, nook and cranny. And—I do not exaggerate—he watched my slightest move. When I inadvertently set my pencil down, he nearly leaped out of his precarious seat.

Had he leaped up, it seemed to me, he would have burst the office at its seams. It looked as though this enormous man had been stuffed into this small room. No building was big enough for him. He needed the out-of-doors. Still he hadn't said a word, but it was obvious that his discomfort was far greater than that of the usual patient undergoing the ordeal of the initial visit.

I tried to ease that discomfort by gently explaining what Jonah could expect. "Now on this first visit, Jonah, we usually try to make a plan, spell out treatment goals, and agree on a plausible way to reach them." I hoped my professional tone would help to calm him. "Do you have any problems with that procedure?"

His eyes grew more wild looking.

"I don't like procedures!" he roared, his voice sounding like the rock crusher in a gravel pit.

So my assumption was right: He *was* going to be difficult! Instinctively, I reviewed my options. The psychology graduate program I had pursued at Nineveh University had trained me for coping with oppositional patients, the kind of people who never want to go along with anyone on anything. But would the rules I had been taught hold good for this disagreeable Hebrew prophet? I guessed he was in pain; that his hostility was merely the way he had of coping with anguish too deep for him to master; that, at the moment, he had no other way of dealing with his misery; and that inside this big man was a small child afraid to reach out to anyone with his pain and panic. If I was right, I would have to meet him where he was—try the head-on approach. "Okay, mister. Why don't you tell me what you want?" With all my experience as a therapist, I couldn't have predicted his answer.

"You're the psychologist," he boomed at me. *"You* tell *me* what's wrong with me." It was a declaration of war! Was he trying to get me to terminate our work on the spot?

I took a chance. "All right, I'll tell you what's wrong with you. You're a troublemaker." I paused, gauging his shock and anger by those wild eyes. The coyness with which some therapists dodge questions would likely inflame his hostility. Besides, a good therapist has to show that he won't have heart failure if the patient is aggressive. "And you're here because you've made such a mess of your life you can't get it untangled."

"What did my test show?" he shot back, suspiciously eyeing the forms I'd laid on my desk. "I spent three hours answering those idiotic questions!"

His *Nineveh Multiphasic Personality Inventory* had indeed generated a profile which suggested a paranoid personality. I wasn't ready to go into that with him at this juncture, and slid a file folder on top of the forms. Regardless of the test results, I had to keep reminding myself that Jonah was in anguish, that he likely felt very small and lonely, and that he was doing his best to camouflage his wounds with a frontal attack.

Nevertheless, I had to run the show. Bitter experience had taught me that becoming timid and deferential with this kind of patient only increases his anxiety and hostility to the point where he will fail to enter into the secure relationship he needs to recover from his illness. Somehow, I had to hook Jonah into therapy before he stormed out of the office. I thought of the next tactic, a risky one: *Face him down. Get him to talk about his problems.*

"I'll go into your tests with you when I think it's time," I countered. "In the meantime, unless you want to ruin another opportunity, start telling me how you came to the point where you thought you needed help."

I could see the red bald spot get redder, and I had no doubt that he was angry. I realized we had rapidly come to that critical moment, which comes in every initial interview, when I needed to establish control—to challenge the patient to get better and wait for his decision. Would Jonah's habitual neurotic maneuvers aimed at controlling every situation take charge of therapy, too, and thereby ruin his chance of recovery? Or would he let go? From the turmoil that played on his face, I couldn't predict which way he would choose to go.

At last he grated out a reply. "I don't like anything you've said to me so far, so why should I trust you?" Belying his belligerent tone, the words held a pathetic plea for help, all the more incongruous in a man his size. He was dodging my challenge. Yet I was not going to let him have the upper hand. I stared back into those powerful eyes. Trust, he'd said. I surmised that trust was no small problem for him. Yet I felt pressure emanating from his powerful personality—pressure to back down, be soft, even groveling; to prove with words that I was caring and trustworthy. Yet I knew that a massive man like Jonah would ultimately despise such softness, and that if I gave in to the pressure, our relationship would be finished before it began. I dared not offer this man anything artificial. You don't create trust in a person like Jonah by faking love or by verbal reassurance. Trust will grow the hard way, if at all.

"I can't think of a single reason why you ought to trust me," I replied directly. "You don't know me. On the other hand, the pain that drove you in here is your pain." I wondered if he would understand what I was beginning to suspect, that the very tactics which had so far kept him from beginning a therapeutic alliance with me had likely brought about whatever misery had driven him in here. I could imagine how difficult it had been for him to come. And I felt certain his disdain was a front for his fear. "You can keep that pain if you want to and maintain your lifelong stance of universal suspiciousness. Or you can take a chance and make a stab at changing some of what's brought you so much hurt."

"How do you know I'm hurting?" he leered at me, still sparring, still trying to force me to talk so he wouldn't have to face the issue of trust.

"No good, my friend," I replied; "the ball is in your court. If you want help, you'll have to get to work. And you'll have to take your chances with me." That he'd hung in with me this long was evidence of his desperation. Still, I was more weary than when we began. I noticed by the clock we were coming to the end of our session.

"I don't *have* to do anything," he bristled.

"You're absolutely right," I came back calmly. "And neither do I. You're a free man and it's your choice—for now." It would be easy to tell this impossible paranoid that I had had enough, that he would have to turn elsewhere for help. Part of him had been trying to get me to do just that—yet I held my tongue, aware of the helpless child I sensed recoiling deep within him.

"A free man? That's a joke. That's the same trap Yahweh sets for me. Every day, He finds a new way to entangle me in His nets. 'Choose,' He says, 'for I have given you a will to choose, but choose my way and mine alone!' You're just like Him." Jonah's eyes began to moisten with angry tears, but he took an iron grip on himself and stopped the tears before they spilled down his sunburnt cheeks. "You say, 'Choose.' But you and I know that I must choose your way. I hate you both."

"Then your anger is at God?" I supplied. Now something was becoming clear. I saw why he had come to me: I was the only psychologist practicing psychotherapy in Nineveh known to be a believer in the invisible God, Yahweh. Some of the others paid lip service to the gods of Assyria, but when you talked to them privately, they revealed their intellectual foundations in agnosticism. They had a solution for the ever-perplexing plight of the person who is angry at his God! Teach him there is no God to be angry at. These psychologists thought they had found an adequate and satisfying answer at the tower of Babel. They were always talking about the potential of man and how it would be fully realized only when the gods were dead. They were priests at the altar of man. They would have solved Jonah's problem by dissolving the Deity, and/or his significance. They would teach him there was no God to be angry at.

Jonah, with his intuition, would have seen through to the end of their logic, and rejected any of those counselors out of hand. I realized now that, as Shem had alluded earlier, Jonah must have tested the waters with a secular psychologist or two. And to have confronted men who insisted there was no Deity for him to argue with must have been maddening for the prophet.

Behind his conflict, he was a follower of the Law, a man

in love with a God he couldn't get along with and couldn't live without. Not a chance that any therapist's spiritual dullness would convince him that God was not real, or that being at war with Him did not matter.

Jonah's eyes had glazed over, and I needed to bring him back from wherever he had gone mentally. I repeated: "You're angry with God?"

His eyes refocused. "He won't leave me alone!" he replied, the agony of his conflict pinching his lips into a thin straight line. "When He speaks, He demands the unreasonable. And when He is silent, even His silence echoes through the hell I live in."

"The hell you live in?" At last I was hearing his anguish. I had to get him committed to telling his story before our time ran out.

"I couldn't go His way with Him, so I chose hell. But He wouldn't let me alone even in the pit. He found me even while I sought a place where He was not."

"Tell me about it, Jonah. Tell me what happened to you," I urged him forward. He opened his mouth, then caught himself.

"First tell me what's the cure," he demanded. (Just when I thought he was hooked!) "I need to know the cure."

"Your story hasn't been told yet," I replied. "Until then, we will not talk about a cure. And even then, it's most often God himself who must heal the disease you have been describing." I stopped myself, not wanting to betray my deepest doubts: I was not at all certain Jonah could be cured.

"I still don't trust you," he muttered. "But at least you don't hand me empty words like the others. We'll see if you can believe my story." His eyes fixed on some invisible point between us. "It begins with hate. I hated the Assyrian empire for oppressing my people into the dust. I believed God loved my people, that He loved me as well until . . ." The gravel-crusher voice slowed to a halt, and Jonah's eyes glazed over again.

Indeed he was hooked—just as our session time ran out.

I picked up on the silence. "Our time is up for today, Jonah. I think we should have another session tomorrow. Then I'd like to see you twice a week for a few weeks."

He blinked, and looked at me. For a moment he wavered. "I don't know. I don't see how you're going to help with this." Then he glared at me accusingly. "Nothing good has happened so far!"

Then: "I'll give it one more session—tomorrow—and see what I think by the end of that one." It was obvious that he was not impressed; paranoid personalities seldom allow themselves to be impressed.

We rose, and I showed Jonah to the door, watching the red, bald spot with its blisters disappear down the hall and around the corner toward the outside door. Then, as I started to shut my door, something else caught my eye.

A man stood in the shadow of a potted palm. As if he had been waiting for Jonah, he watched the prophet pass, then quietly followed him down the hall. In a moment, both had disappeared.

Turning back to my office, I felt barraged by questions. Would I see Jonah again after tomorrow? I wasn't sure I even wanted to spend any more time with this unpleasant man. I reminded myself again that his anger and suspicion were only a defense against his fear and hurt and that, if all went well, he might learn to love and be loved. Meanwhile, could *I* love him? *Lord, if you can love him, you can create the same love in me*, I prayed. But I wondered most of all if Jonah would ever get well. Could a man so alienated from God find his way to peace? I hardly dared hope.

And fleetingly, I thought about the stranger lurking in the hallway. I shook my head. Surely Jonah's mistrust was already beginning to rub off on me. I dismissed the shadowy figure from my mind.

As my thoughts turned to home and supper, one stray, whimsical question glanced through my thoughts: *I wonder what made those white blotches on his skin?*

2

Nineveh University

Death's mightiest pow'rs have done their worst,
And Jesus hath His foes dispersed;
Let shouts of praise and joy outburst. Alleluia!*

Funny, once I'd met Jonah, I suddenly seemed to hear his name mentioned at every market stall and street corner in Nineveh. Squeezing pomegranates at a dingy stand the very next morning, I overheard several tidbits about his exploits from other shoppers.

They were saying that the most unlikely people had turned from their sins because of the preaching of Jonah. It was said that even the slave trader, Tiglon, had divested himself of his holdings and changed his ways.

As I plunked down some coins for my produce, I wondered about Tiglon. How long would his "reform" hold? In fact, I wondered about the others too. Religious fads have a way of coming and going. And I knew from experience that following the ways of the Lord required more than a flash-in-the-pan "experience." Most of all, I wondered how Jonah, of all people, could have won an audience, let alone induced them to change their ways!

On a street corner between my office and the university, I picked up more startling news from the conversation of two undergraduates. Scrolls in arm, they paced along in front of me, and I could not help but overhear when one of them said

---

**Finiti iam sunt prailia*, author unknown, 1695; tr. Francis Pott, c. 1859.

it was rumored that Professors Banipal and Nachar, the twin stars in the heavens of the Psychology Department, had both repented—and that the preaching of Jonah had driven them to it!

One student even described Banipal, roaming the campus in sackcloth, ashes smeared on his brow. I could not believe it—could not even *picture* it. Banipal—the worldly-wise professor, moved by a country hick prophet? How could it be?

And Nachar? The other student insisted that Jonah, exhausted and weary from his preaching, had sought out Nachar for counseling. So *that* was who Jonah had seen before coming to me. I could not fathom Jonah forming a therapeutic relationship with anyone in the university's Psych Department—impossible.

At Nineveh University, the psychologists had become something like the priesthood of a new "cult." They did not preach or proclaim, though; they were much more subtle than that. They insisted they had no intention of interfering with anyone's religion or values—though critics of their work pointed out that they subtly fostered their own man-centered beliefs.

Horrified at such a challenge, the psychologists claimed they were merely technicians of the soul, working to bring about something called "mental health." But in practice, they palmed off their own, often questionable morals and values on students and patients alike. As I said, their methods were subtle.

They began by painstakingly discouraging spiritual experiences of any kind—most of the psychologists who followed Banipal's school of thought, that is. Nachar's brand of psychology had a slightly different stripe, allowing for "experiences of the soul." Somehow, I had suspected that much of their debating was simply for those in the grandstands, because underneath it all, they shared many of the same basic assumptions. And the assumptions were these: Spiritual experiences—those sparked by "religion"—only created intolerable conflict within men and women. They worked to eliminate such conflicts by allying themselves with that part of a client they considered natural and unsullied, striving to bring a person to a state they called "self-actualization." And they felt they had achieved their aim as soon as a patient began to manifest, without inner conflict, the view that he was the center of the universe. Then the therapist considered the patient to have achieved "mental health." At that point, the patient became, in effect, his own god.

That two of the leading proponents of these doctrines had converted was more than my imagination could handle. As I turned onto the street leading to my office, my thoughts drifted back to student days and to the impressions I had formed of Banipal and Nachar, my two most famous professors.

When I was a graduate student at the University of Nineveh, Banipal was the epitome of human intellectual pride. I remember the first lecture I ever heard him deliver.

He strode across the platform that day, with an air of dignity only a professor in the Psychology Department could muster. Psychology was the subject most sought after by undergraduates. They believed, though few would openly admit such a motive, that psychologists could offer solutions to life's problems. And they flocked to psychology courses, assuming that the studies offered at Nineveh's world famous school of human behavior would unlock the door to the mysteries of existence.

Meanwhile, the psychology faculty basked in its prominence under the guise of a modest front, humbly poohpoohing the notion that psychology had the answers. They realized that no one would actually believe their disclaimers, and that they would be viewed as not only the wisest, but also the most modest of the academic specialists.

Banipal, I realized as I watched him perform before his breathless audience, enjoyed his position. In those days, he was the only acknowledged star in the Psychology Department, having published more learned research than the rest of the faculty put together. He loved to lecture on the reasons why psychology was at present woefully inadequate as a science, arguing that the field was in its infancy and that psychotherapy especially had never been proven scientifically to be effective. He flicked his whip of scorn at the draft horses in the clinical division who taught budding clinicians how to make diagnoses and do therapy. In his view they were far from scientifically rigorous in their pursuits.

"Instead of waiting for the evidence to be gathered by painstaking research," he would growl, "soft-headed clinicians simply assume that psychotherapy cures. Now that is a convenient assumption. Pursuing it fills many clinical pockets with hard cash, while, for all we know scientifically, the mumbo jumbo advocated by Lasmow, Gorser, and the rest of the gurus could actually be making their patients worse instead of better!

"There ought to be a moratorium on the production of clinicians!" he would declare, thumping his fist on the podium. "Give those would-be humanity-saviors a rigorous course in experimental design. Let them devote their lives to hard research—then, maybe, someday they will learn something that will really help the poor unfortunates who turn to them for direction!"

And where were students to find this paragon of long-suffering, hard-headed, rational, devotion to pure science? Why, in Banipal, of course. And so he enjoyed the adulation of nearly the entire campus.

"Skepticism, that's what psychologists must learn," Banipal urged the students in his seminars. "Believe nothing until it is proven, and then hold it only provisionally—like this year's overcoat."

The students believed and wrote down every word, determined that they would be lifelong skeptics, accepting nothing as true for longer than they would wear their overcoats. Even when eventually practicing psychotherapy for high hourly fees, they promised themselves, they would not put much faith in therapy—nor in anything else except science. I know this, because I was one of them. At least I half accepted Banipal's thoughts. Of course, each of us fervently hoped that soon psychotherapy would arrive at the status of a true applied science. Then we would be able to believe in it fully, with the same assurance we felt about a science like, say, engineering. It was then I realized lay people already believed that what psychologists did was indeed scientific. As far as they knew, psychotherapy was the only treatment the world offered through which suffering souls could find help.

"Put your faith in nothing except the scientific method," Banipal would finish. Then he would gather his notes and march from the lecture hall amid our stunned, if half-questioning, silence. *Except the scientific method.* There was always that exception, that exemption from the imperative to practice all-embracing skepticism. Occasionally it troubled Shemuel, the one Hebrew student in the graduate school, even as it troubled me. No one ever gave a reason why science should be exempt from the deliberate skepticism with which other kinds of knowledge were met.

Like most graduate students from time immemorial, Shemuel had willingly suspended his religious beliefs when he entered the university. This he told me on our first meeting. He had assumed, because all academia assured him it was so, that he was about to be inducted into new understanding, higher than his "sentimental" childhood faith.

In the Humanities Department, they called this higher understanding social concern, and in the Psychology Department they called it science. But in both departments, it amounted to the same thing: the reverent worship of man. Sometimes this religion is called "humanism," but even then I felt the term misleading for the real object of adoration was to be one's own rational mind. And that god would be ready to receive devotion as soon as one had passed the preliminary examinations and finished the dissertation for the Ph.D. degree. At last, one's intellect would be certified by the other members of the "inner circle" as fully worthy of worship. By that time, we students assumed cheerfully, the faculty would have revealed the answers to all the riddles of life and we would have committed the answers to memory.

"And," many of us must have thought in our heart of hearts, "surely by that time I will understand life on a level of intellectual proficiency undreamed of by my parents, my childhood religion teachers, and the others who shaped the primitive notions about reality which I have heretofore acquired."

I had reached my office, and gently slipped the key into the lock. It was an hour before my first patient would arrive, and the office was still and quiet. Other scenes from my university days began to play in my mind's eye. All the assumptions of "higher understanding" did not go entirely unquestioned. It was Shemuel, or Shem as I came to know him, who first had enough guts to spar intellectually with the old paragon himself, Banipal. Dropping my bag of fresh produce on the papers scattered over my desk, I recalled one lecture-hall confrontation.

Banipal was again lecturing on his favorite subject: how we could make psychology a true science. "And so we must confine our language to words which stand for observable events," said Banipal, "or to terms whose meanings can be derived from observable events. You may have terms in your theoretical network which do not, themselves, stand for anything that can be observed directly. But unless these terms are necessarily related to propositions which can be tested by experiments, they must be viewed as meaningless."

"Professor, excuse me," came a nervous but determined voice from the fourth row. "How can you say for certain that there is no truth to words that refer to things we can't see or touch? Like the Eternal, or the Good?"

"Ah, I did *not* say there is no truth to such words," Banipal parried. "I said they have no meaning, Mr. ah, Mr. . . . ."

"Judahson, sir. Shemuel Judahson. Then, sir, are you saying that things we can never observe with our senses or with scientific instruments *might* exist, but we shouldn't talk about them?"

Banipal was the incarnation of paternalistic patience. "Mr. Judahson, kindly listen to what I am saying. I have not forbidden anyone to talk about such things as the Eternal. However, philosophers have mouthed their speculations for centuries, and no two of them have come to agreement. Plainly, they are using meaningless terms. And their talk is therefore nonsense. Now, if we confine our discussion to observations and measurements of nature and natural phenomena, we can begin to get agreement. That's what science really is—a means of obtaining agreement on what is so."

Shem's face was a study in concentration. "Then you are saying that there is no God."

Professor Banipal rolled his eyes, "Students always have so much trouble accepting the fact that I am only saying *language about God is meaningless*, and that you cannot, therefore, be saying *anything at all about God's existence.* Can't you understand the moment you make a statement about God's existence, you are talking nonsense, using meaningless language? I myself cannot find a way to believe in God, since any statement about Him, being meaningless, is, for me, unbelievable."

"Of course," Shem rejoined, "that includes statements *denying* the existence of God, as well as those asserting it—isn't that so? Thus, the only respectable position to take on that question is agnosticism."

For a moment, Banipal looked ill, as if a virulent germ had invaded his stomach. However, he took control of himself immediately. Too many good minds had followed the "What if . . ." that this untrained student was suggesting, and became mired in the sticky meaninglessness and endless discourse of the philosophers and theologians.

Banipal recovered his patronizing tone. "One day you will find that the only answers come from pure science. I confine my psychological studies to the realm of nature. There is plenty to be learned about that which can be seen and touched, about natural phenomena. And the human mind is only one more natural phenomenon. Knowledge of the mind will come. Why, science has already provided more sure knowledge than all the wisdom of the theologians through all the centuries of human history."

But Shemuel was not to be brushed off. "If we are to be skeptical of everything, why shouldn't we be skeptical of science as well?"

There followed a nervous shuffling of papers throughout the lecture hall. It was dawning on me that, though Shem's position was eminently reasonable, none of our university mentors would be able to see it because they, like other men, were literally incapable of believing in nothing at all. Even those great intellects who were carving out pathways in the science of psychology for us to follow could not really hold *everything* with the tentativeness of this year's overcoat. Doomed by their own humanness, I began to see, they needed a faith in something—and that faith was in nature and science. In fact, teachers like Banipal were not at all skeptical about the ultimate dependability of their own minds. He could not admit—maybe did not even realize—that his fundamental notions were held by faith. His entire belief system was founded on a whopping assumption: that man's intellect is supremely correct, and the only appropriate court of final appeal.

Banipal had totally ignored Shem's last remark, and rolled on with his lecture. However, his questions had given me a new basis for examining the assumptions of others who had been bending my mind, however subtly, to their way of thinking. Now I saw the same "faith" proclaimed in other classes, including those taught by the Psych Department's star-on-the-rise, Professor Nachar. Where Banipal's theories seemed cold and calculating, something about Nachar warmed the heart.

In those days, Nachar had not yet achieved the popularity of Banipal. This may have been because Nachar was not an experimentalist and could therefore not properly classify himself as a scientist in the category of Banipal. Surely the fact that Nachar had never written as much as a single book and had published next to nothing in scientific journals shut him forever out of Banipal's exalted category in academia.

A gentle, smiling clinician with a beard, Nachar always had students waiting outside his office. To him and him alone they dared to bring their problems. It made little difference that he published no research in the columns of *The Assyrian Psychologist*. The other faculty members somehow let you know they were interested in your research, not in your depression, so you didn't go to them with your personal life the way you gravitated to Nachar.

Nachar agreed, of course, with Banipal, that science was supreme. But he allowed himself to believe in a few more things. Man, the most diversified of all the animals, had a brain which, being far more complex than the brains of other animals, made him, Nachar often told us, more valuable than the others.

With my growing insight, I began to analyze Nachar's position. He did not seem to notice that his assertion—that complexity confers worth and value—was no more than an assumption, taken on the same sort of blind faith by which Banipal clung to his assumptions. Besides, Nachar found in man a peculiar self-awareness which made him even more worthwhile. He loved to quote the sage who said, "Man alone asks himself the peculiar question, 'What on earth am I doing here?' "

Nachar stressed one central theory: for each individual, the *self* is the center of the universe. Few students seemed to grasp that none of Nachar's notions about worth and value and what was the center of the universe could be proven or even properly expressed in the object language—the language of science firmly rooted in observable objects and events, nor that these notions could not have arisen from any number of measurements or experiments.

"Your task as a clinician is to assist in the unfolding of the patient's true *self*," Nachar would intone. "Often you will see men and women who are emotionally crippled, their respect and love for the self beaten down. Man must learn to resist all those forces which rob him of the opportunity to realize his fullest potential. Your patients are fundamentally good and full of possibilities. You are to help clear away all that hinders their unfolding into fullest blossom."

Nachar was quick to tell us what some of these hindrances were. "Many have been crippled by the irrational demands of senseless gods," he told us, and his voice oozed compassion for the victims of these demands. "Women have been denied the right to determine for themselves who they will be, or how they may use their own bodies. And men— men have been forced into a mold, compelled to compete, pushed to be aggressive, and made to shorten their precious lives trying to live up to the foolish demands of a so-called 'masculine' image."

Students all around me wrote furiously, not wanting to miss a word. "Not all religion is evil," Nachar allowed. "Some have discovered god within themselves. This discovery of the god within is the primary growth experience. But we must oppose the old tales of gods who issue senseless demands that prevent the unfolding of our true selfhood.

"Such gods force people into nonsensical molds. Sexual molds, for example. We must remove the barriers to full and manifold expression of that love which is a natural outgrowth of our humanity. Of course, the expression of love is often, perhaps most often, sexual." (I noticed that the note-taking slowed a bit, as the audience absorbed this attractive idea.) "And it is senseless to force sexuality into some sort of channel, preconceived for mankind by priests. In our clinical work, it is our duty to shatter those molds, break the fetters; then discover in what direction each individual is unfolding, and gently facilitate the emerging of the person—also with regard to the expression of love in sex."

I could tell by the expressions of some classmates, they had just resolved to make freedom of choice, sexual freedom—and every other kind of freedom—available to all their clients and to themselves, too. Never would they allow such a growth-stifling emotion as guilt; never would they entertain the heretical thought that what they were doing might be wrong; never would they commit the cardinal sin of living a life that was unfree. And the supreme goal, Nachar finished, was to pour yourself into the work of preparing to free others.

I glanced over at Shem. Even he seemed enrapt in Nachar's words. I decided to seek him out later.

Since the day Shem had confronted Banipal, we had talked a good deal. Both of us were in our second year of graduate school in the clinical program, and were preparing for our preliminary examinations to be taken in the spring. As we talked, we had discovered that both of us were becoming uncomfortable with much that we were hearing.

My own views had been influenced heavily by my father, an Assyrian government official who had managed to survive without yielding to the pressures of state religion—that total devotion to the emperor expressed through the cult forms of our national religion. Although my father had never discovered a positive alternative, he communicated his skepticism of the nature gods and emperor-worship to me. It was natural for my skeptical attitude to extend to the scientism and man-worship which was apparently the semi-official religion of academia.

Through my new friendship with Shem, I had made the most important discovery of my life: I came upon the Hebrew Scriptures. There I found the true God. The more I read of these holy books, the more convinced I became that Yahweh ruled heaven and earth, and that a man could do no better than to spend his life seeking the face of the Lord. Before I realized what was happening to my skepticism, I became a believer and came to know Yahweh as my own God.

Shem, ironically, was not quite ready to concede to the truth in his own heritage. So I'd found myself in an amusing reversal: an Assyrian, trying to convince a Hebrew of God's existence. That was where all our talks had brought us.

On the afternoon following Nachar's latest lecture, Shem sought me out. Knocking on my dorm-room door, he poked his head in at the same time. "Got time to talk?"

"Sure."

Sprawling on the bed opposite me, Shem opened in his usual, forceful manner. "Banipal is an absolute jerk."

"So is Nachar," I added, knowing, but not sharing, Shem's admiration for him.

"But Nachar is different. He cares," Shem insisted. "Banipal doesn't love anybody but Banipal."

"Shem, have you ever thought about the love of Yahweh? Really thought about it?"

"Aw, come on! You're not going back to that Yahweh stuff, are you? You know that's primitive. No rational person can believe in the existence of tribal deities today." Shem sounded like the success of the anti-Yahweh movement depended on him alone.

I ignored his attempt to rekindle an old argument. "Remember how Moses wrote about the love of God? That love spoke to him out of a burning bush!"

"Of course I remember that story. Next thing you'll say is that you believe it happened!" When he said that, his lip curled, with obvious disgust for the direction the conversation had taken.

"That story should make you think," I pursued. "You know how Banipal is always saying religious stuff isn't anchored in observables? That it's all nonsense statements? His favorite example is, 'The Eternal flows on timelessly.' And there he's right. That kind of statement *is* nonsense. But, Shem, we've uncritically accepted his notion that it's that sort of meaningless abstraction we encounter in the Torah. And, Shem, it isn't. It isn't at all. The burning bush was no abstraction. It was right there in front of Moses. He saw it. He felt its heat. If he had had a thermometer he could have measured it. If that bush hadn't been observable, if Moses hadn't been able to see and hear the acts of God as He commandeered natural objects for His purposes, Moses would never have accepted God's commission to lead Israel out of Egypt."

Shem was pondering this, I could tell. And I pressed my point. "And think, Shem, of the giving of the Law to Israel on Sinai. Those people experienced observable events of all kinds, including the dividing of the Red Sea and the annihilation of their pursuing enemies in the returning waters. Shem, that's not the way Banipal likes to tell us it is. Whether the Torah is true or false, its teaching is *not meaningless.* It's all based on observable events, the actions of God in His world of natural objects, as well as in human lives."

"But," objected Shem, who was not without his own doubts about Banipal's philosophies, "Nachar is different. Doesn't your own heart tell you his teaching on love and freedom must be true?" Something in his tone begged me to share in his admiration for his mentor.

"It sounds good, Shem, until you look at it closely," I replied, determinedly. "But once you have—"

Shem interrupted me, shouting, "It *is* good! Nachar is a loving man who knows the way to human freedom. We can't give up on him, too."

"But think of Yahweh's love," I reminded him. "How different it is from Nachar's. In the Torah, Yahweh's love saves

His people from their captors, and sets them free to love and serve one another and their children. Yahweh's love gives them the law with its instructions on right and wrong. Within its limits man can live. Outside its limits he is not able to live for very long, so he dies. By contrast, Nachar's kind of love sets people 'free' to end up in his bed." (Shem almost interrupted, but stopped himself. We had both heard the stories of women *and* men students who had learned about "sexual freedom" with Nachar.) "He thinks he has freed them when they renounce their obligations to any rule but his rule. And who reaps the ripe, young fruit of Nachar's labors? Nachar does. How different from the love of Yahweh!

"Another thing," I hurried on, as Shem shook his head uncertainly, "Yahweh's love doesn't promise freedom from obligation. It promises fellowship with Yahweh. It doesn't offer self-actualization, delivering the self to the self. It offers the self something greater than self, and in submission to that greater One, a different kind of freedom than the one which lines students up at Nachar's office door and lures them into his bedchamber."

Shem was wavering—I could see it in his eyes.

"In the end," I said, "both Banipal and Nachar preach the same thing: worship yourself. Banipal favors the intellect, while Nachar makes his feelings and his sex drive into deities. But they both work to make converts for the same religion: one in which man is his own salvation."

After that day, Shem and I began to study the Torah together. Though there were no questions on it in the preliminary examinations, we became convinced by semester's end that here was Truth higher far than Banipal's "truth," and love and freedom far beyond anything Nachar had ever imagined.

Oh, yes. Shem and I came to believe that the burning-bush story really happened. It had to have happened, because without it there is no cogent explanation for any of the rest of the tale.—And, finally, for the rest of the truth of the universe as well.

Those were the days when I had time to wonder about "Truth." Time to challenge the philosophies of even the most renowned minds. And now, on the streets of Nineveh, they were saying that Banipal and Nachar were talking of new things: of sin and repentance. How was that possible? Because of one abrasive, traveling prophet. Even the cult prostitutes in the temple of the goddess were said to be hurting for business!

If these things were true, what power could have brought them to pass except the power of a living God? Even if the reform didn't last, it had to be a miracle. Undeniably, such changes as Banipal's wearing sackcloth and ashes *are observable*! On the other hand, whatever had happened to Nachar through Jonah's preaching had not been enough to prevent his therapeutic tactics from alienating the Hebrew prophet.

The thought made me uneasy. If Nachar's was not a true conversion, what about the others? As I sorted through my papers, preparing for my first appointment, I wondered, momentarily, what would happen to Jonah—a hero at the moment—if this spell of mass conversion were to break.

3

Whither Shall I Flee from Thy Presence?

Jesus lives! I know full well
Naught from me His love shall sever;
Life nor death nor powers of hell
Part me now from Christ forever.
God will be my sure Defense;
*This shall be my confidence.**

Jonah's appointment time was four o'clock. I knew he would arrive early—if he came at all. If he didn't keep his appointment, I would be free of this man and his war with the invisible One, a war I did not especially want to be involved in. But He was in pain, and, apparently, God had sent him to me.

Evidently, I was spending a lot of emotional energy preparing for Jonah's return visit. All throughout my morning sessions, I had to fight to keep my mind on the patients' concerns. By noon, I felt drained and, rather than taking a lunch break, I shut myself in the office, drew the window blinds and lay down for a quick nap—something I rarely did.

Fitfully, I dozed, conscious thoughts about my new patient weaving and blending with strange dream images.

I was in a pitch-dark cavern in the heart of the earth.

Jesus lebt, mit ihm auch ich, Christian F. Gellert: 1757; tr. Frances E. Cox, 1841, alt.

Though I could see nothing, I somehow realized that another man was there with me. I didn't know him from Adam. Though I had never seen him before, there was something about him that seemed familiar. He never moved, never opened his eyes, never spoke. At last I realized that he was dead. I knew too that I shared his fortunes, as if his death was, oddly, my death too. Was I dead as well? What was I doing in what was evidently a tomb? While I pondered this, the rocks suddenly split, the earth shook, and through a great wide opening, streams of golden light poured. My companion, now alive and gleaming with the brightness of the morning star, walked out through the torn earth, beckoning for me to follow.

When I woke fully, I felt disturbed. Although I was accustomed to interpreting dreams during psychological treatment, and although I frequently analyzed my own dreams, there was something different about this one. It was unlike the usual night dream which must be written down immediately to prevent loss of its details. This dream was as starkly vivid upon waking as it was during the dreaming. And I encountered only frustration when I tried to interpret it. I couldn't discover where the dream material originated, nor could I connect it with the events of the previous day. No amount of free association produced anything with the ring of truth.

It was only when I'd decided to give up struggling for meaning and went over to reopen the window blinds that a flash of insight startled me. From where, I could only guess, a blaze of words formed in my mind: Something in Jonah's life—something that felt like death and rising from the grave— was actually maneuvered by God as a sign; he was only a foreshadowing of a greater Prophet who was to come.

If the dream's interpretation was clear, there was still an enormous amount of confusion on my part. Why should I have received this insight? What could I possibly do with it? Immediately I sensed that Jonah would probably be enraged if I so much as hinted that he might be part of a higher design.

In fact, I was not very comfortable with the feeling that *I* was being drawn into some powerfully whirling vortex. To what end? I did not know.

As I came to the end of the clinical fifty-minute hour with my three-o'clock patient, I felt anxiety growing in the pit of my stomach. His name, Jonah, meant "dove." Somebody had to be kidding when they named him. Noah had sent the dove from the ark and she had returned with a sprig of green— "good news, the flood is over." Jonah's nature was anything but dovelike, and as for bringing good news, he had brought Nineveh news of her coming destruction and me nothing but worry. Part of me hoped he rather would be like Noah's raven and simply fly away, never to be seen again. I realized that I was afraid of Jonah, afraid that he would bring me more to deal with than I could bear.

Moreover, the wish to be rid of him and his problems caused pangs of guilt. After all, he was in trouble. It was my job to care for him, to be an instrument for his healing.

As I escorted my three-o'clock patient to the waiting area, I vowed I would make myself and my skills available for the working of the Spirit of the Lord. But I knew the God with whom Jonah was so furious would have to do the work.

Jonah was there all right. He had even arrived early. Perhaps now I would learn what he was so peeved about.

"Come in, Jonah."

He followed me into the office, and sat down without a word, waiting for me to begin. The expression on his face dared me to help him: He stared me down without flinching.

"At the beginning of each session, I will ask you for feedback on the previous session," I began nervously. "What I want to hear from you is any reaction to what we did. Anything that was helpful, anything that was painful, any reaction at all to the session we had yesterday is what I want to hear." I expected more of the verbal whipping I had taken the day before, but was somewhat amazed when he actually tried to follow my instructions.

"You put me in a bind," he began. "I don't want to talk to you. I thought I could get you to do the talking, defending yourself or explaining yourself or something. You wouldn't go for it. I still don't trust you. But you were right. What choice do I have? I have to talk to somebody and you're my last chance. It's not much, but it's all I have to turn to!"

He's hooked, I told myself, both exultant and panicked. *For better or worse, he's my patient now. God help us!* Still I remained silent, as a therapist must if he wishes to teach the patient to do the work of getting well.

"You've probably heard of me," Jonah continued matter-of-factly. (I smiled impassively.) "I'm the man who arrived here six weeks ago, predicting that Nineveh would be destroyed. At first, your compatriots made fun of me, accompanying their taunts with ripe vegetables. 'And are you going to unseat the emperor, monarch by his own might over all the earth, Grandfather? Go back to the woods; you'll never make it in the city!' They had a lot of fun at my expense.

"I was furious, but I'm not flexible. I don't turn easily from the course I've set for myself. I walked through all the settled area between the rivers, crying out, 'After forty days, Nineveh will be destroyed.'

"No, I'm *not* flexible. And I was determined to reap a reward for my trouble. If Yahweh was going to destroy these murderers, I was at least going to get the message out first. Yahweh's idea of justice is too liberal. He always gives the criminal far too many breaks."

"But they listened," I interposed.

"Yes, they listened," he fired back. "And that's the worst part. I didn't want to come to Nineveh to begin with. Assyria deserves to be—*must* be wiped out! If you could only see what her armies have done in conquest and I fear will do to my country." Now his words became angry—stabbing. "Why should I, a Jew, be forced to aid in the rescue of such an instrument of evil? Yet I was forced to come. *Forced.* I had to speak in the streets. My last hope was that they would close their ears and die.

"Why did I come? *He* left me no choice." At this, Jonah's bulging eyes glanced at the ceiling accusingly. "Yahweh had used me to deliver His commands before. Each time I knew the cause was just. But not this time! This command scalded inside me. How could I, a true patriot, preach repentance and deliverance to the military power that held my people in its clutches? I didn't want to be used to help save this citadel of the world's worst evils. Can you tell me Nineveh *shouldn't* be destroyed? Of course you can't!"

I was determined to remain detached, therapeutically neutral, but I imagined Jonah could hear the loud thudding of my heart. "You believe Yahweh spoke to you directly, then?"

He laughed bitterly, as if I had made myself the object of any right-thinking person's utter scorn.

"Believe Yahweh spoke to me? The *Word* of Yahweh *came* to me. You egg-head types sit around all day talking about the truth, and you think the truth is something you'll discover by a mental quest. You pore over your clay tablets, you make your rats run their mazes yet another time, and the more useless facts you learn, the further the truth slips from your grasp. From time to time, you stumble on something you think is worthwhile. Then you try to make yourselves believe you've found truth. But you're embarrassed to say point blank about anything, 'This is truth,' because your fellow intellectuals would laugh at such gullibility. You're afraid they'd tease you for swallowing a nursery tale.

"You can't go on a quest for truth. Either you *know* the truth or you don't. If you don't know it, you won't recognize it when you find it. And if you do know it, you don't need to search for it."

I was amazed at Jonah's powers of expression and grasp of spiritual concepts. His rough exterior cloaked a fine mind.

"The truth is *alive!*" he exclaimed, slapping his knee for

emphasis. "Truth is a Person. He comes to you. You don't go out and discover Him. And when He comes to you, He comes to take you captive. This Word *comes*. You don't sit around discussing with your cronies whether you're going to agree. You either go with God, or, if you are a stubborn fool, you do your best to get away." The fire in his eyes dared me to argue.

"And you—surely you obeyed His command?"

He only glowered at me.

In the silence, as Jonah paused to catch his breath, I had a moment to consider what I'd just heard. With my own retiring disposition, I could not imagine anyone daring to act in direct opposition to what he believed was a command of the living God. But Jonah, I now understood, had done just that. He had plainly heard God's bidding and refused it—had met the flint-hard will of God and turned from it. He had known the love that comes to seek and find, and yet willed to be lost.

Jonah was telling me of a love that had come after him, that it might give love to him, as well as to Nineveh. The love Jonah was talking about entered the universe from without. It came to transform, and it would not be deflected from its purpose.

With that thought came a crystallizing idea: I had never realized before how assertive God is. We psychologists often tried to help our patients to "speak up," to deal assertively with others. But now, as I listened to Jonah, I saw God as the divine Model. For He speaks plainly. I have encountered clients who were in a tizzy because they did not know God's will for their lives. These people made a great fuss about their titanic struggles to discover what God wanted them to do—as if God were so shy He barely hints, or speaks with such a weak voice He can hardly be heard, with the result that it is up to man to decipher the meaning of God's diffident little whispers! Jonah was showing me how wrong is this view! He spoke of a God who makes His will known loud and clear unless you stuff your fingers in your ears. Of course, He may reveal only a step or two at a time, a frustration to those who insist they need to see the whole journey from the very beginning.

Before I could follow those thoughts further, Jonah cleared his throat, and continued his narrative.

" 'Get up,' Yahweh said to me. 'Go to Nineveh . . .' This was no hint. Not a divine suggestion. Not, 'You really should try Nineveh; you'd like it this time of year. After all, it's a place you've never visited. Perhaps if you went and met the people, you would understand them. You would see that the Assyrians are ordinary folks just like you. Then you would stop hating them so.' He didn't ask me. He told me clearly. And I stopped my ears. *I disobeyed Him.*"

I was shocked—not by the sarcasm, because that seemed to be directed at the Assyrians, not Yahweh—but because his words were so bold and simple. Jonah did not pretend, like so many, that he hadn't heard clearly. When God says, "I want you to . . ." and then follows it with a command we don't agree with, like, "Give up your plan to marry so-and-so," or "Stay with a man who doesn't love you because you are married for life," many say, "What's that? I don't believe I've heard you, Lord. I just can't figure out what the will of God is." But Jonah was not wishy-washy enough to sit on any fence. He heard and he *knew* he heard. And he said "no" point blank.

"I decided to get away," he continued, "—away from Him and his commanding Word. Nineveh lay to the east, so I booked passage to Tarshish and boarded a ship bound for the west. I turned my back on Nineveh—and on God, too." His eyes glazed over, and I sensed he was again on board that vessel bound for Tarshish, fleeing from the presence of the Lord.

It was at this moment I realized something was happening

inside me. During psychotherapy, peculiar changes some-times occur in the attitude of the therapist. The most unat-tractive patients begin to appear beautiful. Their most out-rageous acts become, not merely understandable, but even excusable in one's eyes. And so I found myself mentally de-fending my patient's disobedience! He had, after all, been motivated by love for God's own people, Israel. He did not play dishonest games like so many professional purveyors of religion.

Still, he was suspicious of the motives—even of God, and that is a great iniquity. And because of that I could not come up with an adequate defense for Jonah. He knew God, but he could not believe Him. He was sure the God he served was going to rip him off.

"Why?" I asked—the therapist's favorite question. "Why did you not trust Him?"

His eyes grew dark with bitterness. "I knew what He would do."

"So?" A simple prompting for him to continue, but, he took offense.

"*So!*" he shouted at me. "Don't you understand, you thick-headed, overpriced parrot? I knew I couldn't trust Him to follow through and obliterate the Assyrians. I knew I was being used as a tool by which God would love my own en-emy!"

I ignored the angry put-downs. "You thought you could win an argument with God by running from Him?"

"I only knew I couldn't go *with* Him." With that he set his jaw. The humorless face became impassive, stubborn. More strength than I had would be required to pry those lips open.

"Jonah, our time is up for this session," I said, feeling that I had utterly failed to come up with a thoughtful, brilliant interpretation that draws clients back to the office to continue their work. I wouldn't have been surprised to have been in-formed that I had not met his qualifications for continuing.

His response was surprisingly docile. "You want to see me in a week, then?"

I took advantage of it to advance the work a bit. "No, I'd like to see you *twice* a week for a while. Can you come in on Monday?"

"Monday—at the same time? I'll see you then," he said, rising. He lifted his hand in what was meant to be a farewell wave, and exited the office.

When he was gone, I breathed easier—for a time, that is. All weekend long, two fears fought with each other inside my breast: fear that Jonah would not return, and fear that he *would*. I asked myself day and night, "How do you help a man reconcile with God when he has declared war on his own salvation?"

I could hardly wait for Monday; yet I feared it would come too soon.

4

Shem

Jesus lives! For me He died,
Hence will I, to Jesus living,
Pure in heart and act abide,
Praise to Him and glory giving.
Freely God doth aid dispense;
This shall be my confidence.*

Although anxious thoughts about Jonah were not far from my mind all weekend, there was something that made me look forward to Monday morning. On Saturday, Shem was going to be in Nineveh on business, and we were to meet at my office. Since he had taken a position in the Psychology Department at Babylon College, I hadn't seen much of Shem. This would be an excellent opportunity to consult with my old friend concerning this difficult, new patient.

And there was one other topic that occupied my thoughts: Nineveh—this great center of our empire, the hub of the world—this "citadel of evil" as Jonah had dubbed it. Nineveh is a huge city—or rather, a complex of cities, a great metropolitan area at the confluence of the Tigris and the Upper Zab rivers. While Nineveh proper is three miles long and a mile-and-a-half wide, the area known as the "great city" includes other towns and villages nestled together in a megalopolis. That blending of cities and forces had made Nineveh strong, so strong that our leaders often said it was our "duty"

---

*Jesus lebt, mit ihm auch ich, Christian F. Gellert, c. 1757; tr. Frances E. Cox, 1847.

to extend "help in governing" to surrounding nations. It seemed a good policy to most of us in Nineveh. Yet Jonah's complaints had made me see that others did not necessarily welcome this, our "foreign policy." Jonah had said Assyrian forces had "set the very earth on fire." That troubled me, but I did not know what he meant.

On Saturday morning, however, brighter thoughts seized my attention. I kissed my wife, Miriam, and the children, and set out to walk the mile or so from home to the office. As I strolled in the warm, clear sunshine, I continued to ruminate about Jonah and Nineveh. It would have taken the prophet several days to cover the city on foot, stopping here and there to shout his peculiar message. He must have seemed so out-of-place to the 120,000 jaded, sophisticated Ninevites all around me. The fact that most of them had dropped to their knees was not merely incredible—it was beyond my under-standing.

It was halfway to the office, in midstep, that the remark-able thing happened. For one breathless, splendid moment, it was as if curtains opened and I caught a glimpse "inside" nature. For a split second, I heard the sound of trees clapping their hands, mountains and hills shouting for joy, creatures chattering their praises to Yahweh as they performed their lowly tasks as acts of highest adoration.

And there I stood, gaping on a busy sidewalk. When I snapped-to, I realized that passersby were giving me wide berth as I stood stupified at all this transcendant beauty. It hardly mattered what they thought; like the dream that had come to me several days before, I was receiving wisdom from outside myself. This time, though, I thought I knew what it meant: Despite Jonah's anger and clamor for justice, despite the things the Assyrian military had done—whatever that might be—there was something "higher" at work here. Some plan Jonah was not aware of. Nor was I, for that matter.

I saw another thing, too. Banipal and Nachar had missed

the truth about nature: It was not a closed system. Theirs was a lock-tight, cause-and-effect universe; nature was just a meaningless series of events. But they had missed the truth. Nature was alive and noisily grateful, shouting the praises of her King.

And though I did not know it at that moment, this uncanny glimpse of the higher purposes—even for the fish in the sea, and the trees and plants of the field—was to become a key that would unlock the mystery of the events surrounding Jonah. And my unwitting part in his story.

When I met Shem at the office, I did not speak of the "opening curtain." Jonah was the pressing concern for me just at the moment. As soon as Shem and I had cuffed and embraced one another, I poured out the story of my unlikely patient and his even more unlikely Ninevite congregation. One of the more unlikely results of Jonah's prophesying Shem had seen for himself, for he told me he'd visited Professor Nachar at the university. Shem was having difficulties of his own trying to explain the evident sincerity of Nachar's repentance. And he'd heard that Banipal, too, had come under the prophet's mysterious influence.

"The spell has enthralled more than those at the university," Shem said excitedly. "This morning I passed the Temple of Ishtar. You know it's ordinarily packed with 'worshippers' on their way in or out of the chambers of the goddess' surrogate lovers. It was deserted and the love chambers were locked. They say even the emperor has donned sackcloth," he marveled.

"Shem," I responded, "if I had not seen Jonah, I'd agree more readily with your conclusion that God is behind the impact of his preaching. But I have talked with him. A more *unlikely* prophet is difficult to imagine."

"Does God need a likely prophet to do His work?" Shem countered.

"How could God pick out so hate-filled an instrument?

There must have been others in Israel who could have brought some of God's love to Nineveh. Yet Nineveh has been spared, and that is surely an act of God's love," I conceded.

"Maybe God doesn't need human faith and trust before He can accomplish His purpose through a human being," Shem responded. "Could it be that He needs nothing at all? That He can perform His purpose through even the most resistant and rebellious instruments?"

"Why not? Why should the Lord of hosts not use means which, from man's point of view, seem entirely unsuited to His purpose? Of course He could, if He chose! Of course He could, Shem. And in Jonah's case, He evidently did."

For a time, Shem and I fell to talking together about Jonah's psyche. I needed this professional consultation.

"He's angry because he believes he was forced to preach here, in a city he hates more than he hates his own misery," I explained.

"Who doesn't become angry when he's forced to act against his heart?"

"No, Shem, it's deeper than that. This is not just a case of God riding roughshod over the human freedom Nachar loves to talk about. Jonah can't and won't put any trust in God."

"Has he ever trusted Yahweh?"

"I don't know," I replied. "It sounds as though Yahweh simply compelled him to come here. I don't know how. Coffee?" I had brewed a fresh pot, remembering our late-night cups together while studying for exams.

"Thanks. No cream." He sipped thoughtfully. "I don't like all this talk about Yahweh forcing and compelling him. It violates man's freedom of choice. What ever happened to free will?" I noted that he was still absorbed with Nachar's notion that every human being has a free will and should be permitted to choose his destiny. Nachar was fond of citing research results which demonstrated high correlations between authoritarianism and such psychological flaws as aggression and violence.

"Free will?" I echoed. "I didn't know free will had been demonstrated. And if you were a thoroughgoing scientist, careful to stay with the evidence, you wouldn't so much as mention the term. You know very well that the research we have suggests that man's behavior consists of responses to stimuli. That means behavior is determined by stimuli. Determined, Shem! Logically there's no room for the notion of human freedom. You know B. F. Thinner's argument against human freedom and dignity."

"Oh, for heaven's sake, wait a minute, will you?" This was a familiar argument between us, and Shem was ready to battle. "I know Thinner's theory. And I know how you and Banipal argue for it. But neither of you ever lives by it. Did something make you take a sip of coffee just then? Or did you decide to do it? You talk about choosing and deciding, and it would be utterly out of the question for you to talk or think if you didn't. Why do you live and speak as if you had choices and were free to make them if you really believe otherwise?

"Furthermore, it's not true that evidence shows behavior is not freely chosen. Determinism is an assumption—and a totally useless one, since nobody lives a day in his life without making choices by virtue of his God-given free will. Thinner's book is nothing more than an appeal to the scientistic ambitions of psychologists. They want to be just like physicists. The joke is that while some psychologists agonize over making the study of behavior like physics, physicists formulate theories attributing something suspiciously like free will to the particles which are the building blocks of matter—"

"Get off your soap-box for a minute," I interrupted, "and I'll agree with something you said." This argument was so well-worn by now, each of us knew his next line. "I have to agree that Thinner and other behavioral determinists may be going too far. I *did* choose to take a sip of coffee. And, so far as I can tell, I choose many other things. But what about the biggest of all issues? That's one I have to hand to Jonah. He wouldn't waste an instant worrying about a theory of human freedom. But what does worry him is that God permitted him no choice in the matter of Nineveh. When I listen to his story, I wonder, is our response to Yahweh a matter of freedom, like taking honey in a beverage? Can a man choose God freely, without force or compulsion from God himself? Could Jonah?"

"Of course," answered Shem. "That's what gives meaning to life. You choose your ultimate concern, your god. Everyone does, except the man or woman who just exists like a vegetable. You and I have chosen Yahweh. Others decide to pray to Ishtar. And others make science their highest good, the ultimate concern for which they're willing to live or die. Jonah has chosen Yahweh, just as we have, although he may be struggling with his choice right now."

"I wonder," I replied. "I wonder if Jonah is the one who made the choice. It looks to me as if it is God who does the choosing. Look at the Torah, the writings of Moses. What does the Torah say? There is no doctrine of freedom of choice even hinted at, is there, Shem?

"Oh, I know there are commands to choose between the way of life and the way of death, between Yahweh and other gods. But a command doesn't necessarily imply that one has the ability to obey it. For instance, God commands perfection, a thing which no man has ever been able to achieve. About man, to whom you attribute such freedom and dignity, Torah says he is dead as a result of the one truly free choice he ever made. He decided freely to eat the fruit God had forbidden. He was never free again. Can the dead raise themselves? No. You can journey down the Tigris and see the Babel Tower—or its remains. That aborted monument to pride symbolizes what happens when the spiritually dead try to raise themselves to the heights where God dwells."

"Then how does anybody ever come to know Yahweh?" Shem appealed. "You and I made a choice for Yahweh back in graduate school. We came to Him. You remember how it was."

It was a powerful argument. We both thought of ourselves as having made a choice for Yahweh. We had felt as though we were choosing. But why did we make that choice? Why did Banipal and Nachar suddenly wear sackcloth, though it was not "in" for academics this year. Could it be that our wills had been given something, some help from outside, to enable us to do what we never could have done unaided? Could it be that we were raised from the dead? Not by our own reason or strength, but by a life-giving Spirit?

I remembered something my paranoid patient had said. "Jonah told me that the Word of the Lord *came* to him." I tried to recapture the essence of that discussion. "He said it was not like his trying to seek out God's will. Certainly it had nothing to do with Jonah's *choice.* It was more like he had been trying to get away when God's Word came like an electric spark, jumped the gap to wherever Jonah had crawled to hide himself, and singed him with its energetic heat.

"Still," I continued, "it appears Jonah made some sort of 'choice'—granted, it was the wrong one—because he deliberately bought a ticket and boarded a ship for the opposite side of the world after Yahweh ordered him to Nineveh."

"*What?*" Even Shem believed point-blank rebellion was carrying the issue of freedom too far. I knew that his own submission to Yahweh had come rather smoothly, on the heels of conviction. There had never been a fierce struggle for him, except for a few misgivings about what his decision might do to his chances for an academic appointment at Nineveh. Perhaps for both Shem and me, the whole issue had been settled a bit too easily.

Really, now, I thought, *Yahweh has never commanded us to do anything we resented doing with our whole hearts. Does the fact that the issue has never reached a crisis for us mean that we are less rebellious than Jonah?* I wondered. Perhaps the "choice" of man, unaided by God's Spirit, was *always* to turn 180° away from Yahweh's path.

"You can understand, Shem, why I don't know what to do with this man, can't you? It's as if I am being called in to finish something God began in him, and I don't understand what I'm supposed to do." I suppose I wanted Shem to tell me.

He nodded. "It's as if you are being written into a play you never chose to act in. And you have to wait for the author to give you your next lines," Shem admitted. "Doesn't sound much like free choice for you, either, any more than for Jonah. But if he said 'no' to God, how did he ever survive to tell about it? It was my impression that God reacted with swift wrath to prophets who refuse His will. And how on earth did Jonah come to preach in Nineveh if he took ship to Spain?"

"I don't know—any more than I know how Banipal, Nachar, the emperor, and the rest of the population of this Sodom-on-the-Tigris could have been turned inside out by one seemingly deranged paranoid. Shem, I don't know if he *can* get well. And the more I hear of his story, the more implausible it all seems. I don't really know what I'm expected to do for him."

"Yes, you do," Shem replied gently. "Well, at least you know enough to take one step. Agreed, you don't see the end of the matter between you and Jonah. And it's true his recovery is *very* doubtful. But you *do* know that with any paranoid patient, you must let the relationship develop to a level of trust. Without that, you'll accomplish nothing. In fact, you'll make matters worse. If Jonah can come to trust you, his anger may give way to acceptance. Perhaps then he will let you look at his wounds.

"Meantime, your role is to steer clear of the holes Jonah digs for you to fall into. You know he'll take pains to provoke you. Part of him wants you to get upset with him so he can walk out and say you've confirmed his belief that nobody can be trusted."

I set down my empty coffee cup and let out a deep breath. This helped. I knew some of these things, but I needed to be reminded of them. I had wanted to know much more: I wanted an explanation for what I did not understand, and direction for where I was to go with the rough-clad stranger; to know there was hope in treating such a man. I did know this: Jonah both loved and hated God. To heal Jonah would mean healing a raw wound in his spirit, the mortal sickness of his separation from the One he loved.

Shem couldn't come up with even a guess about the cause of the spots on Jonah's skin. After a few more moments of lighter banter, Shem and I parted, he to return to Babylon, and I to meet my family for a picnic on the river. Monday would be here soon enough, and I needed relaxation.

As I walked home through the quiet streets, I pondered what my friend had suggested for me. How could I develop trust and preserve it in a man who seemed determined to interpret everything anyone did as a violation of his personal rights? That Jonah went around with a chip on his shoulder was not especially surprising to me. All paranoid patients did that. What could I do to convince him that I would not betray him? I knew the answer: Speak nothing but the truth. I must not give in to the impulse to try to look more amiable, friendly, and loving than I really felt, for his piercing eyes would see through a false front instantly. With Jonah, as with God, I would have to walk in integrity, or suffer the consequences.

"Lord, I do not pray to be used," I whispered as I neared home, "for you have thrust it upon me to be used. I simply admit that I am without the resources to meet this man's needs. Lord, you have written this play and your choice has cast it. Please give me my lines. Amen."

5

Away from the Presence

It was a strange and dreadful strife
When Life and Death contended;
The victory remained with Life,
The reign of Death was ended;
Holy Scripture plainly saith
That Death is swallowed up by Death,
*His sting is lost forever. Hallelujah!**

On Monday I found myself checking the hallway before Jonah's session. I half-expected to see that stranger lurking as before in the shadows near my office door. But there was no one. Anyway, why would someone be interested in following Jonah? Surely not for the purpose of robbing him. I noted, as he followed me into the office again, that he didn't have anything worth taking.

"You haven't let me tell you my story," Jonah accused me sullenly after he had stalked into the consulting room and claimed his straight-backed chair. We were entering the rainy season and, outside, the sky was cloudy and the air heavy. *Appropriate*, I thought ruefully, *for Jonah's mood.* He was already attacking and blaming me for something before we had even begun. What would the rest of this hour be like?

I wasn't going to defend myself, but I wasn't about to cave

---

*Christ lag in Todesbanden, Martin Luther, 1524, cento; tr. Richard Massie, 1854, alt.

in to his hostility, either. Our relationship was fragile, and I was watching over it like an eagle brooding over her single nestling. Very simply, I replied, "Tell it."

"Where did I leave off?" he murmured.

I knew the ploy. Patients had used it times without number. Translated into ordinary speech it means, "Show me that you care about me by remembering what I said to you a few days ago. You see so many people. Am I just a number to you? Or do you value and love me enough to remember me? Does my pain matter to you?" Jonah was beginning to care about our relationship; a thin span of trust was beginning to bridge the chasm between us. I was ecstatic.

I was also wary. I did not want to reinforce his efforts at manipulation. And even more important, I wanted to let his interest in my feelings toward him do its salutary work, prodding him out of self-absorption into healthy interplay. No point in rushing in with reassurance. So I kept silent.

"You don't remember!" he bellowed, accusingly.

Still I continued my silence. *Remember?* I mused. Who could forget? All weekend I had tried to guess how Jonah, on a ship to Tarshish, had come instead to Nineveh, a spot on the earth that lay in the opposite direction from Joppa where he had taken leave of his own land. But silence can be a powerful therapeutic tool, if the therapist can control himself well enough to use it.

Unnerved by my steadfastness, Jonah shifted in his chair, tried staring me down, and finally decided to go on. "I think I told you I had boarded a ship for Tarshish to evade Yahweh and His outrageous command—" He hesitated, waiting for me to confirm his statement, still pressuring me for assurance that I did remember, that I cared. I was tempted to take the bait and nod, but I kept to my resolve. No reassurance—not yet.

After another moment's hesitation, he continued. "I usually have trouble sleeping. But down in the hold of that ship, perhaps because of the rocking of the waves, I fell into a sound sleep. The weariness of days and nights without rest locked me into a prison of deep slumber. If only I could have been kept a prisoner there forever!"

I couldn't believe it. Jonah's rigidity was beginning to crack, allowing feeling to show through—yearning, sadness. His wistfulness meant progress! It was more than I had hoped for so soon from this stubborn, defensive package of hostility. I began to feel a glimmer of hope. Maybe, just maybe. . . .

Unfortunately, I smiled faintly. Jonah, studying my face for clues to my inner response, evidently thought I was amused at his sudden vulnerability.

"Quit staring at me, will you?" he snapped.

With that, he put me in the double bind paranoids are so adept at fashioning. If I didn't look at him, he would accuse me of inattention; if I looked him in the eye, he would say I was persecuting him. I simply replied, "Certainly," and shifted my gaze.

Still I could feel those bulging, penetrating eyes as he continued. "Where was I? Oh, yes, I was in the hold, sleeping soundly. But I was not to be allowed to rest. *He* found me and renewed His efforts against me. Where could I escape from His presence? He hurled a great wind at the ship. We were going to sink. The captain came and woke me, demanding that I join the whole company to pray for deliverance from the storm. 'Call upon your god!' he ordered. 'Maybe your god will give a thought to us so we don't perish.' Little did he realize how I hoped that the God I knew would *not* give a thought to us, or even take notice of my hiding place.

"But the sight that greeted me up on deck turned my stomach. These wild mariners had suddenly become more religious than priests. There is nothing like the threat of disaster to bring men to prayer. I could hear the names of all sorts of gods being hailed, over the howl of the wind and the creaking of the ship's timbers. The sailors had already thrown the cargo to the waves in an effort to lighten her. But nothing helped.

"The waves were pounding the hull—timbers were cracking. They cast lots to discover what *I* could have told them from the beginning. I knew that God was after *me*. I heard His voice above the shrieking wind and ear-splitting thunder. Evidently He was prepared to drown them all to force His will on me." He paused. "I suppose you think I'm paranoid."

I tried not to flinch. What he said was true. Being a scientist, I thought that the storm wasn't anybody's fault; just a natural phenomenon. Jonah was paranoid enough to believe that the Lord God had concocted the storm in order to "get" him. But right now I wasn't interested in discussing Jonah's diagnosis, or the causes of storms. I wanted to hear his story all the way through. So I waited in silence.

Again, it unnerved him. "Don't you ever say anything? What am I paying you for, anyway?"

Still I resisted him, maintaining my silence as I waited him out. With a disgusted look, Jonah went on with his story.

"Anyway, the lot fell where I knew it would: on me. I thought about my situation. Here we were, all of us, about to go to the bottom with the ship. There was no hope for anyone. And, clearly, there was none for me. God had determined to take me, though I had tried to escape. He would never let me go. I knew my persecutor had won. 'I am the cause of the storm,' I told them. 'Throw me overboard, and the sea'll quiet down. Then you'll be saved.' "

This time I nodded, though impassively. Paranoid ideation? It certainly sounded like the notions of grandeur and self-importance many paranoids exhibit. Severely ill paranoids believe they are so important as to be sought out by kings and gods for special persecution.

Why did I reject Jonah's explanation?—I wondered, as he went on. Banipal had taught me to, of course. He would have said, with unconcealed disdain, that one would find it more fruitful to study the winds, the tides, and the temperatures as causes of storms than to attribute them to divine intervention. But I had come to reject these same scientific notions when Banipal applied them to human behavior. If I rejected his strict determinism in regard to man's actions, why should I accept it in the case of nature? Could not nature respond to the will of her Creator just as directly and immediately as a human being? I thought of the moment, two mornings before, when I had experienced nature praising God as if it were a living, responsive organism. In that brief instant I had realized that there was something more to nature than a system of mechanical parts. Wasn't Banipal's axiom that all events have natural causes merely an assumption? Of course it was. No one had ever proved it and no one ever would. At any rate, it was evident that my patient had absolutely no doubt that the sole cause of his storm was Yahweh. And Yahweh's purpose: to have His way with Jonah. I was beginning to feel that somehow, Jonah's assessment might be more authoritative than that of Professor Banipal. Banipal, to my knowledge, had never offered his life in order to save anyone or even to back up his theorizing! He would have considered that the act of a fanatic. Yet this huge patient, doubled over with his anger, was continuing to tell his story with quiet cogency. He had offered to die to preserve the lives of others. How unlike what I should have expected of him.

"At first they ignored my solution," he said, with a wry, bitter smile. "They rowed with all their might. But He fought them. The sea grew worse and worse. Their arms gave out. Then they knew there was no other choice. The sailors cried out to Yahweh for forgiveness, and threw me overboard. I could not swim. I plunged down through the black water. It seemed forever. Then, kicking and struggling, I managed to fight my way to the surface just once. The sea was already smooth. The wind had stopped. I thought I might splash my way to a piece of wood from one of the chests the sailors had thrown overboard. But my Assailant had other plans. I turned just in time to see it coming. A sea creature, the size of a ship, was racing toward me, its mouth open. Screaming in terror, I was swallowed whole.

"I managed to breathe by keeping my head above the acidic fluids in the creature's gut. The stench was so overpowering, I argued with myself before I drew each breath. Finally, I decided to inhale through my mouth, but the sour fumes hurt my lungs.

"The darkness was total," he continued, his voice sinking to a hush. "The noise all around me was like that of a huge machine. The thud of the creature's heartbeat, the swish of blood, the body fluids, and bubbling gasses hummed around me, hurting my ears. I knew nothing but terror.

"My recollections from this point on are cloudy. It was as though I was buried alive—in hell without having died—and nothing could get me out. Terror overwhelmed my anger, and desperately I called out to God—even though, only a few hours before, I wanted to escape Him forever."

I realized I was gaping. Evenly, reasonably, this man was spilling out the most *un*reasonable story I'd ever heard. Fortunately, he was not requiring a response, but continued without pause.

"I don't remember much else. I'm sure I was in a semiconscious state most of the time. Near as I can figure, I was in the belly of that thing for three days and nights. During my lucid moments, I cried out to Yahweh.

"And do you know the worst of it? The fish became sick of me and vomited. I was forced up through that massive, slimy digestive tract and catapulted onto a sandy beach. I thought I was free. Surely God was now ready to let me go. What an act of mercy and love, I thought, to free me from my suffering. But I was wrong. He had freed me only to force me back into the vise.

"He broke into the very praises I was shouting to Him,

and dashed my heart with His command: 'Get up and go to Nineveh. Preach the message I will give you.' " (Here, he seemed to be taken by a stomach cramp as he clutched his abdomen.) "And now you know the cruelty of my Adversary."

So saying, Jonah fell silent. The angry wetness crept back into his eyes as he stared out the window. For a moment I tasted his pain; warm compassion was welling up inside me. I noticed a new feeling toward Jonah: My fear of him was shrinking and my love for him beginning to grow.

For a moment my intellect swayed: How could I believe him? I would be a poor scientist indeed to swallow such a tale. To accept his account as truth would be stepping inside Jonah's psychosis with him.

But I did believe him. Why, I don't know. Just a half-hour earlier, I thought him totally deluded. Now I was responding as if this were the Word of Yahweh himself. Somehow, when he finished, I *knew* that, at least in this instance, Yahweh had hurled and recalled a storm and prepared a fish to swallow a prophet because He had chosen to do a work in Jonah and the city in which I lived.

Now, too, I knew what had caused those splotches of white that discolored his skin.

At long last, I broke my silence. "It must have felt to you as if God was determined to shatter you!"

"I know He was—and still is," he replied, dropping the defiance I expected.

"Still is?" What else had God done to him?

"That's what I said, 'Still is'! And if you're going to call me a liar, you can keep your 'therapy'!" (He said it like that, so I could hear the quotation marks around "therapy.")

Shem had warned me to beware of these provocations, so I didn't let myself react. I held my tongue, and I concluded we had come far enough for one session.

"Perhaps this is a good point at which to stop for today," I replied, not wanting to reinforce his anger, but having no heart to rebuke him for it either.

The fact that I was neither smirking at him or gratifying his story with a pitying expression seemed to disarm Jonah. If he wanted a strong response, he had been disappointed. Lumbering to his feet, he kept his eyes on me all the way to the door, as if he expected me to laugh the moment he turned his back.

His hand on the door frame, he stopped and continued to stare, as if his eyes could bore a hole in my head and see my thoughts. *Must hold steady*, I counseled myself. One false twitch—one smile misread and he'll never come back. Carefully, my face rigid, I said, "See you next time."

Then his eyes released me. The balding, white-splotched head disappeared into the hallway. I sank back in my chair exhausted.

"O Lord," I found myself praying, "can it be that you have set out to destroy that man? What evil has he done? I want to believe you for his healing. Please give me enough faith for that. Surely, Lord, if you could turn Nineveh upside down through his preaching, you can draw even Jonah to yourself."

In a quiet place within, I was given to know the response of the Almighty: *What makes you think his end is destruction? Haven't I brought him to you?*

"I think until now I have puzzled about who or what brought him," I heard myself mutter. "Please, Adonai, my Lord, direct me."

6

The Jonah Committee

Lo, Judah's Lion wins the strife
And reigns o'er death to give us life.
Hallelujah!
Oh, let us sing His praises!*

The Jonah matter was not far from my mind during the days between sessions. Not that I was unable to think about anything else, or to give thoughtful attention to my other clients, but my thoughts kept coming back to the most extraordinary drama I had ever been given a part in: the struggle to the end between Jonah and God.

As best I could gather in our next few conversations, the struggle had arrived at a standoff. Jonah wasn't backing down, and neither was Yahweh.

Well, perhaps Jonah did back down—to the extent that he had walked through Nineveh, grinding out his message of doom begrudgingly.

The swath cut through our populace by this man's preaching was broad indeed. Already, though, some were beginning to weaken in their resolve.

Some came to regret the high cost of moral and spiritual change, forgetting rather quickly the salt tears of repentance they had shed a few weeks before. Many on the psychology

---

**Aj, ten silny lev udatny*, From the Bohemian, c. 1650; tr. John Bajus, 1940.

faculty of the University of Nineveh began to consider their reputations in academia and found the sweet savor of intellectual respectability more to their taste than the bitter ache of the penitent's broken heart.

Furthermore, rumors were beginning to circulate. I heard them through my wife, who kept her ears open at the market. Some who had repented and now regretted their repentance had lost money and were even plotting against the prophet. Could this have anything to do with the shadowy figure I saw following Jonah as he left my office after his initial interview? I wondered if Jonah was in danger.

Still, though most were returning slowly to their old ways, other Ninevites were still genuinely interested in pursuing godly lives. *Apparently* so, at any rate.

All this became more distressing to me when I considered that the prophet had not wanted God to spare Nineveh. Jonah would have loved nothing better than to see his message, which he had dutifully proclaimed, ignored by my countrymen—to our immediate doom!

Yet there had been repentance—or the appearance of it. And Nineveh was spared. Now, however, the repentance was crumbling, and Nineveh seemed to be scot-free of any judgment. To Jonah's thinking, he had every right to be furious, to challenge and struggle with God.

What frightened and amazed me was one nagging question: Why did God allow the struggle to continue? When I considered what Yahweh could easily have done to him, I feared for Jonah. How long would He, whose power knows no bounds and whose wrath had once destroyed a prophet for doing no more than staying overnight in a forbidden place—how long would such a One continue to strive with this man? He could have unmade the prophet when Jonah ignored all reasoned argument, insisted on quarreling over every inch of the terrain across which the Almighty had dragged him so far, and turned his suspicious questioning even on the loyalty of God! I shook my head when Jonah, in effect, dared God to wipe him out.

And whenever Jonah talked about the flabby "conversions" of the Ninevites, the veins on his forehead pulsed. "Wasn't this what I predicted?" Jonah crowed, repeating his conversation with God for my benefit. "I knew you were soft on sin! That's why I didn't want to come here in the first place. I knew you would make a fool of me. And that is precisely what you have done. Take my life. I'm better off dead than alive in a world so starved for justice."

I shuddered. God had barred Moses from the promised land for no more than striking a rock with his staff. Why didn't He visit this man's insistent rebellion with instant death?

As a matter of fact, God's reply to Jonah, as he reported it, seemed to me a model of restraint—a good model, I thought, for any counselor working with an angry patient. Softly, gently, the Almighty simply asked Jonah a question: "Do you do well to be angry?"

That was the last straw for Jonah. He had stalked out to the east of the city. There he built a small hut of branches, and sat in his shelter to wait and see what would become of Nineveh. He told me—and again I shuddered—that he was just waiting for God "to come to His senses and rain fire on the whole town."

If I'd thought earlier that Jonah might suffer delusions of grandeur, I was tempted to think that again. Now, instead of claiming that God was persecuting him, Jonah insisted that God was performing all manner of miracles to show Jonah His love!

Wild as it sounded, Jonah rattled on that God had caused a gourd plant to grow up *overnight* to shade his miserable little hut. He claimed it was ten feet tall and that it protected him from the fierce Mediterranean rays of the sun. Now I almost regretted believing his story about being swallowed by a sea creature.

Still, there was something about this gourd-story. The gourd, Jonah insisted, was appointed to minister God's mercy to him by its luxuriant growth of shady leaves. But Jonah, still intent on seeing God's wrath break forth, refused to bend his anger. He riveted his unblinking eyes on the heavens over Nineveh, tense and intent on seeing his own will done.

On Jonah's next visit, the deep fury was back: The story got worse. God, who had made the gourd for Jonah's protection from the blistering heat, also fashioned a worm. The worm's task, in happy accord with its nature, was to devour the sheltering plant so that it withered. So effective was the little worm's appointed ministry that overnight the grateful shade dried up.

Again Jonah was left sitting in the sun, his hut affording little defense against its aggressive rays, or against the hot east wind. The already-damaged skin of his scalp fried in the blazing heat.

When I suggested he ought to move in out of the heat and spare himself some pain, I thought Jonah would burst.

"I'm not moving!" he bellowed. "I'd rather die!" Jonah was shouting at me exactly as he had shouted at God when, as he reported it, the Almighty had asked: "Do you do well to be angry for the plant?"

Jonah had long ago thrown caution to the winds, and, having marinated himself in the vinegar of self-pity, he screamed like a child having a temper tantrum, *"I do well to be angry, angry enough to die!"*

When Jonah told me how God had replied, I could almost feel the ache in the loving heart of the Father for this recalcitrant son, for Nineveh, and for me, too.

"You pity the plant," God reportedly had said; "yet it was not yours and it cost you no labor or time. It came and went overnight. Yet you accuse me of injustice because I pity that metropolis down there, more than 120,000 persons who do not know their right hand from their left"—the next words touched me deeply, for they showed the meticulousness of God's caring—"and also much cattle."

What a gentle God, I mused while Jonah seethed. What gracious concern. What a loving reply! Not a word of reprimand for Jonah's rebellion and stubbornness. Just a soft admonition for his lack of love. I wondered if prior to meeting Jonah, I hadn't missed this order in God's priorities altogether.

One night during those strenuous, tiring visits, I dreamed again. This time, I was in the presence of Him whose train filled the room. He was holding a meeting. "I am appointing a committee to take action in the Jonah matter," He announced. "You, Storm, and you, monstrous Fish, I appoint you both to the Jonah committee. You, Gourd-plant, you serve too. And you, little Worm, will go also and do as I will instruct you." Then He turned His face toward me. "I appoint you, Psychologist. You will know what to do when the time comes," He said.

Then I woke in the darkness of my room. I woke with a new insight about the storm, the sea creatures, the gourd and the worm. Each of them had been a glove over the hand of God, a committee member appointed to begin a new work in Jonah. However the natural scientist views the matter of cause in nature, it was clear to me at that moment that each created being must be capable of casting loose from the system, free to be used by its own Creator.

Another wry thought took me. How many such committees are there? Was there a committee appointed to deal with me? Could someone write a story beginning, "And God appointed a prophet. And the prophet came to a psychologist to vent his furious wrath . . ."?

Perhaps.

One thing seemed certain, as I punched my pillow and tried to relax again: Ill-at-ease as I felt, I knew that I, too, was on The Jonah Committee.

7

Nachar on Love

Here the true Paschal Lamb we see,
Whom God so freely gave us;
He died on the accursed tree—
So strong his love!—to save us.
See, His blood doth mark our door;
Faith points to it, Death passes o'er,
*And Satan cannot harm us. Hallelujah!**

Shortly after I began my work with Jonah, a young woman named Rana, a student at the university, began to see me for depression. She was a lovely blond woman, with dazingly golden-brown eyes. Just now, those eyes were flat, expressionless.

Like Jonah, she, too, had had a disturbing experience with Professor Nachar. However, it was not because she had sought treatment from him. No, what she sought was something quite different. And it was her encounter with the old clinician that had precipitated her illness.

Her volume of words, considering she was suicidally depressed, was really quite amazing. On her very first visit, a remarkably long story flowed out of her carefully painted lips.

This, I learned, was how it all happened:

Rana had spotted Nachar one evening after supper, strolling along the quads and archways of the university campus. Some of the finest artists had contributed to the beauty of the

Christ lag in Todesbanden, Martin Luther, 1524, cento; tr. Richard Massie, 1854, alt.

school's architecture, and Rana, like Nachar, loved to wander among the flower beds of an evening.

When she saw Nachar, she told me, she was reminded of something he had said just that afternoon in class—and she was struck with the thought that they must be soul-mates. Especially, she thought that when she watched him, believing he was unobserved, stoop and cup a rose in his hands and breathe deep of its perfume. Rana just *had* to ask him the question that was burning within.

"Professor Nachar!" she had hailed him. When he turned, she had been afraid for a moment that he did not recognize her. After all, she positioned herself three times a week in the front row of his lecture class, right where he might note her attentiveness. His puzzled look, she was glad to see, had warmed to one of recognition.

"I'm Rana—I'm in your psychotherapy course," she supplied, not wanting to risk the chance that he, in fact, might *not* know her name.

"Yes, my dear," he eased her fears. "I know who you are."

She smiled, gratified. Why did she feel as if his eyes were wandering over her? She admitted to me it was not an altogether uncomfortable feeling.

She joined him, and they walked along the bank of the Tigris River, which cut the university campus in two. The evening was mild, and the last rays of the sun reflected off the surface of the water, Rana reported, a subtly romantic lilt creeping into her otherwise flat-sounding voice.

"Professor, I've been wanting to ask you something. May I?" she asked.

"Certainly, Rana."

She felt oddly warmed by the way he used her name. Her arm brushed against his as they walked—whether accidentally or on purpose, she admitted, she did not know.

The detail with which she recalled their ensuing conversation told me it had a powerful grip on her.

"Your lecture on the therapeutic power of love today seemed to have been inspired," she said. "I must confess I've never thought of love as therapeutic before. But one thing was not clear to me. When you spoke of love, you didn't mean to include—well, physical lovemaking, too, did you?"

"No question about it, Rana," he replied casually. "The most therapeutic of all experiences is the joining of two persons in that mystical, erotic communion we call sexual lovemaking. All relationships derive from it, and all life energies flow toward that fulfilling moment when lovers lose their personal boundaries and, releasing all of self, flow unstintingly into one another!"

"Only, of course," she put in, "when two persons have been joined in marriage by the priests."

"No, Rana. Priestcraft has nothing to do with love," Nachar quickly replied. "Two souls, offering themselves to one another, need only bring love. Whether they be man and woman, man and man, woman and woman, or even adult and child, the love they share is a natural sacrament. It works its own creative miracle without the mumbo jumbo of the temple."

"How beautiful you make it sound, Professor Nachar. If only . . ."

"If only what, my dear?"

"Oh, nothing. Well—do you recall what you said about Dr. Lasmow's self-actualization theory?" She forged ahead. "You seemed to say that each of us must move in the direction of fulfilling our potential and that this was what psychological health meant."

"That is what I said. It is the peculiar merit of Dr. Lasmow's work that it emphasizes the innate goodness and beauty in the human soul and assigns the therapist the task of bringing that potential into actuality. In other words, the therapist is like a midwife. He is not to create the child, but to assist in the bringing forth of that which has already been planted in each individual from the beginning."

"But what about sin?" Rana's pretty face, even as she pored over the conversation again, was troubled. "What if the person, in actualizing herself, commits evil acts, or does harm to herself or others? Don't we have to say no to some of our deepest inner strivings lest they bring forth wickedness?"

She seemed to be asking the question of me, just as she had sought an answer with Nachar. I did not interrupt, however, to give my response—and I already knew what Nachar's would have been.

"The true inner self knows nothing of wickedness," he told her, "except that suffered at the hands of repressive societies that resist the unfolding of the lovely blossom of individual self. Marriage, for example, is a teaching that comes from the priests, who fear for the livelihood they would most assuredly lose if human beings became free to love. What a crime that the young have been so needlessly retarded in their growth! And all because of repressive notions about the supposed wickedness of the perfectly normal desire of each free soul to meld into meaningful unity with other whole selves."

Without hesitation, Rana admitted the effect Nachar's words had had on her. The great mistake was that she had admitted it to him.

"I do so want to grow as a person," she said, unblinking. "And I yearn for the unfolding of my soul in the reality of love of which you teach!"

Now Nachar's hand found her arm. "Rana, we are so close to my house. I was just going to have a glass of wine. Would you care to join me?"

That evening, Rana could hardly believe that her uninitiated person had been chosen to become united in depth with so great and humble a teacher. What she could possibly offer him she had no idea, but she poured all her youthful passion into her loveoffering to Nachar. And so the night passed.

Early next morning, before the first light, Rana had floated back to the apartment she shared with three other women. In a marvelous daze, she showered, put on her makeup and dressed in fresh clothes. As she walked to her first-hour class in statistics, her mind was busy applying what she had learned. She was now in meaningful unity with another, and that none other than the great professor, Nachar of Nineveh! How glorious was the song of the birds, the smell of the morning air, the light beginning to tint the eastern sky! He had been right! One *did* come into a new dimension of self-unfolding from such experiences. "Nachar, I love you!" she wanted to shout. She now knew real love, meaningful love, for the first time.

She barely managed to keep her mind on the statistics lecture. She had never liked the course, and she liked it even less that morning. What did it have to do with reality? With life? With love? With anything that mattered at all?

Rana, she told me in the course of her long ramble, had chosen to become a psychologist because she yearned to find "reality." (I listened, noting the apparent connection, but waiting for some deeper revelation from the digression Rana led me down.) She had been her father's darling, but had known little other than conflict with her mother. Her mother seemed to be deeply jealous over her father's admiration and affection for Rana. In turn, Rana hid from her uneasiness with her mother in the sheltering arms of her adoring father. There she knew herself to be loved and secure, and it was those familiar good feelings she sought always to relive. She had long identified those particular feelings as "reality." Like most graduate students in psychology, she had analyzed herself that far.

As a soon-to-be professional, Rana told me as she gathered some dignity about her, she wanted to involve herself fully in human concerns. She longed to spend all her time working with people and doing the sort of therapy she imagined really explored the very depths and brought out the total wholeness of the person. She yearned to make people better, to give them joy in living.

The immediate problem was that Nachar, her god, had shattered her.

Finally, Rana came back to her main story, about Nachar. When the statistics lecture had finally dragged to a close, she rushed out of the building and over to Nachar's therapy class.

When the great man, with whom she had actually spent the night, ascended the podium and opened his notebook, she believed she would be transported to the heavens! But why did she get the feeling, from the moment he walked into the room, that something was wrong? Nachar never even looked her way. She had wondered if he would ask her to come forward after class, or perhaps to see him in his office. Instead, he ended his lecture, closed his notebook, and strode from the room. By the time Rana reached the hallway, he had disappeared.

How could anything be wrong? Perhaps he was protecting the intimacy of their love, and did not wish to be seen interacting with her in public. That was it! She would go to his office.

She waited her turn. They needed the privacy of closed doors and freedom from the pressure of other students waiting. The hallway to Nachar's office door was furnished with four chairs. All of them were occupied by students wanting to see the professor for advice, information, or simply the beaming love he exuded. It was a long wait, but at last her turn came. She was nervous, unsure of herself. She walked in and sat down. Nachar didn't look up from his work, but he knew she was there.

"Yes, Rana? What can I do for you?" he said, eyes still on the paper in front of him.

"I—I—I don't know. I came because of last night," she stammered.

"Oh, yes. Last night. So what can I do for you, my dear?"

Still he did not look at her. His voice expressed nothing, as if the night before had been a thousand empty years ago.

"Nothing," she whispered as she pulled herself from the chair. Hiding her tears with her hands she stumbled out of the office, down the hall, and out of the building.

Rana became my patient when, shortly after her appointment with Nachar, she threw herself into the Tigris. A fisherman, who probably never in his life thought for five minutes about the meaning of love or self-actualization, pulled her from the swift current. He saved her life.

And now I had two patients who had, for different reasons, fled from Nachar's ideas about love. Jonah, because Nachar's system could offer him no way to resolve his love-hate struggle with God; Rana, because it could not help her cope with her hunger. Would God give me something to meet both their needs? Vaguely, I sensed some connection between the two—but what?

I was beginning to feel more than a little overwhelmed.

8

Right Is Right and Wrong Is Wrong

Tell me, ye who hear Him groaning,
Was there ever grief like His?
Friends through fear His cause disowning,
Foes insulting His distress;
Many hands were raised to wound Him,
None would interpose to save;
But the deepest stroke that pierced Him
Was the stroke that Justice gave. *

Something about my sessions with Rana and Jonah kept forcing one question to the surface of my conscious thoughts: Was *I* angry with God? At the moment, there were no stresses, no unsolvable problems causing me to struggle with God, to question His love for me. But there had been a time, a period in my life when I shook my fist at the heavens in fury.

Though my problem, a suddenly broken engagement, a betrayal of love, had passed when I met and fell in love with Miriam, something *had* changed inside me. It was this: I had come to understand the many, many patients I encountered in my practice who complained that God was dealing with them unjustly. Most needed little encouragement to express their anger at God. What has been referred to, of old, as "the fear of the Lord" did not seem to give many of these irate folks any pause. As I said, I could understand *most* of them— but not all.

---

*Stricken, Smitten, and Afflicted, Thomas Kelly, 1804.

Rana, for example, actually made me smile to myself when she had left the first counseling session. I sat alone, shaking my head at the vast contradictions she represented.

One of the last things she said to me was, "I don't understand why God takes away everything I ever really want!" She'd complained, "He can't be very loving, in spite of what they say."

Like many who are angry with God, she had not assigned God a significant role in her life before this present crisis, nor would it have occurred to her to consult Him prior to her brief, sad venture into Nachar's bedroom. Nonetheless, in the hour of her own loss and need, she had come to hold the Deity responsible for her crushing hurt. Like many others who have been hurt, she became suddenly religious in a negative direction; her religious feelings were all bitter. But perhaps even angry recognition of God is better than deleting Him from consciousness altogether. An angry sinner is at least aware of God's reality!

Why is Rana furious with God? I mused in the stillness of my office. *It was Nachar, her idol, who hurt her, and she who chose to let him. God did nothing to create her tragedy. What is it in man that prompts him to make a mess and then point his shaking finger at the Deity?* Adam did it, I concluded, as do a great many of his descendants. Even the atheist argues against the existence of God with such ill-concealed rage one wonders if atheism isn't just another form of anger. Aren't many atheists angrily trying to murder God by eliminating Him from His own universe? I puzzled over the alacrity with which people blame God for events which could more easily be laid at the door of someone else—very often the blame-giver himself.

Like Rana, and others who come to the clinic with deicidal ire, Jonah too believed that God had miscarried justice.

Coincidentally (I supposed), I fell into a schedule with these two that put them in my office on exactly the same days of the week. No wonder, then, that the topic of "anger with God" took up so much of my thought life; I was getting a double dose of it.

It was Jonah, of course, outspoken as he was, who kept the question burning. In fact, as our relationship slowly deepened to include what, for Jonah, amounted to trust, he let out even more anger—more than I imagined possible.

One afternoon, in fact, he stormed into the office, slammed himself into the straight-backed chair, his face alarmingly red, as if it would burst with rage. There were no opening gambits.

"He had no right to force me to do this," he charged, his moist, red-rimmed eyes contrasting with the harshness of his gravel-crusher voice.

"You'd be happier if God had not brought you into His plans for saving Nineveh," I reflected back, in order to keep him working on his alienation from the Lord he really loved.

"Of course! How would you like to participate in a plan to free the man who would kill your son? That's how it was for me to be asked to rescue Nineveh."

"You fear that the Assyrian army will eventually destroy Israel?" I asked, naively.

His face purpled. "Have you ever seen what your Assyrian troops do to their vanquished enemies? They whack off the hands or feet of civilians, or cut off their noses, or put out their eyes, or so disfigure their heads and faces as to permanently display large areas of the skull.—No, they are not 'gentle.'

"And neither will be the Assyrian conquest of my country." His anger was now accompanied by deep grief for his people. "They will do as they have done to other nations— carrying thousands away into slavery, importing thousands of aliens with strange cultures and hideous gods and settling them in Israel to defile our sacred soil." At last, Jonah had responded without taking his customary adversarial potshot at me.

"You had hoped God would fight for your people? That

He would destroy Assyria instead of showing her His mercy?" I ventured.

"Hoped? We have the promises! The promises, man! He has promised to fight for us. He has promised His mercy will triumph and that His people will be victorious. Of course there are times when we deserve His judgment," he conceded, "and He has then justly brought the heathen down upon us for our sins. But Israel will turn back to Him. She always repents, sooner or later. She is His chosen one, the Bride of Yahweh." His evident pride was born not of arrogance, but of a confident assurance of the truth.

"And it's so unfair of Yahweh to turn the mercy He's promised to us upon Nineveh which, of all cities, deserves mercy least! It wasn't *just!*" he shouted, punching the word. "He violated His promises!" His sunburnt skin radiated anger as he glowered at me. It seemed as if, at that moment, he was glaring into the face of his divine Adversary.

"It must be painful to feel so betrayed," I responded, without condemnation. (Did I fear his becoming exasperated with me so much that I avoided condemning him for his sinful and dangerous challenge to God? Should I have said something like, "Jonah, don't you know it is wrong to be angry with God?") What rolled over my awareness then was the pain he felt—the pain anyone must feel when he believes God has betrayed him. The ancient, despairing death-cry, "My God, why have you forsaken me?" came to my mind for Jonah.

It was in that moment that, for the first time, I understood him. I was amazed that I felt a deepening love for this bitter, confused prophet. I could not condemn him.

Besides, Jonah was finally letting the wall of his defensiveness come down. And behind the crumbling wall of his old defensiveness, I viewed his desolation. "I have never felt so lost," he was saying in a subdued tone. "God won't talk to me. I don't know if He listens. My guts wrench. The blood pounds in my head. My hands clutch and my muscles contract of themselves. It's as if I'm trying to capture my Persecutor and hold Him until He hears me out.

"It was bad enough that He commanded me to go. But He wouldn't be content with that. He robbed me of freedom. In the end I had no choice—*no choice.* When God robs you even of the freedom to disobey, you are left with nothing. He's stolen your very humanity. I asked Him to let me go, and instead He buried me in the heart of the earth."

Even I was startled at the challenge I levelled at him abruptly. "Jonah, why have you come to me?"

"I—I don't know," he stumbled, caught off guard. "I don't have much faith in psychology or psychologists. I don't know what I expect you to do. Maybe—maybe this is helping some, I'm not sure. I know when I'm here, the pain is less."

I was delighted. I knew that patients experience improvement from simply telling a therapist their feelings—catharsis, psychologists call it. But this was progress indeed!

"You're saying you'd rather stop feeling those knots in your stomach?" I prompted. It did not work.

"Nobody's going to change God or turn Him from His path. He does exactly as He chooses. *No matter what I want!*" he shouted.

Once again I tried, calculatingly, to precipitate a critical moment. "I didn't have in mind changing Yahweh," I replied mildly. "What would you think about changing you? You don't have to stay all twisted up with rage, you know."

Jonah flared at me. "What's the matter with you, you charlatan? Can't you see the truth when it sits on the end of your nose? What's *right* is *right.* What's *wrong* is *wrong.* You aren't going to change that, if you try to twist my head around for the next millennium. Yes, sir. Justice and truth are justice and truth, even if God has forgotten them."

"You feel you can't give in on a point of justice?" I was, at that point, very thankful for the technique of reflecting back what the client had just said to get me through this tight spot.

"Right is established by the Law," he shot back. "It's God's own Law I'm asking Him to uphold. He has commanded justice. Any earthly prince committed to justice would listen. Why doesn't He?"

"And what if God continues to refuse you?" I asked. "What then?"

"Then I want to die. There can be no meaning to life in a world without justice. If God himself is unjust, then the center of all is chaos."

"This can't be the first time you've ever heard of God's patience, Jonah. Why are you so surprised?" I asked, wondering at his utter commitment to justice without mercy.

"Of course I knew before I left my country He was patient—far too patient. That's why I tried to escape to Tarshish. Who, knowing Him, would not have predicted He would find a way to let Nineveh live?" Now it was clear that Jonah actually hated God's love and grace—at least when shown to those he deemed "unworthy."

Briefly I thought of those who say the poor should starve because they are lazy, those who can't wait to stone the fornicator and excommunicate the divorced, who show their piety by refusing to speak to those of whom they disapprove.

This time it was Jonah who ended the session, gruffly noting that the clinical hour was over. The anger he had come in with had turned into disgust; that, plus the fact that he seemed so eager to stalk out in a huff concerned me. The last thing I wanted was for him to abandon therapy now over a point of theology!

Perhaps what happened next was a product of divine humor.

As we made our way through the waiting room, Jonah passed by Rana, who was waiting for her session to begin. He would never have noticed her—but she leaped to her feet, brightening visibly when she recognized him.

"Oh, Mr. Jonah!" she began, charmingly effusive. "I'm so surprised to see you here. I've been wanting to meet you. Everyone's been talking about the wonderful things you've done for Nineveh. I saw you only once, from a distance, and—"

Jonah turned on her, a flurry of irritation and disgust. "I don't know you—and I don't care to. Get out of my way!" He strode to the outer door and slammed it behind him.

As soon as Rana and I had taken our customary places in the consulting room, she burst into tears. "He hates me, doesn't he? I don't understand. What have I done to him?" (On top of her recent rejection by Nachar, this!) "Why is everybody treating me that way lately?" she sobbed.

"Everybody?" I queried, trying desperately to get in control of the situation. I hadn't expected to be catapulted from one tough session into another with no break at all.

Rana did not answer immediately. She sniffeled, took a tissue from the box and daubed her carefully mascaraed eyes.

When I suggested she was associating Jonah's treatment with the abuse of her professor, she nodded. "I just can't find anyone who will love me. I feel so alone!"

It was common for me in clinical practice to encounter people with erroneous beliefs. Many patients believed they had to make everyone love them. But with hysterical types like Rana, winning the loving adulation of men—all men— seemed the imperative. For her, accustomed from childhood to being adored, especially by her admiring father, any sign that an adult male could not be captured was a source of turmoil.

"Why is it so important for you to have Jonah's love?" I asked her.

"I don't know—it just *is*!" she responded petulantly.

"Then tell me this, Rana. Why should Jonah and Nachar and the rest of the male sex automatically love you?"

"That's just the way it's always been. I've always found

that men liked me a lot. I need it."

"But, Rana, has that kind of love really blessed you? What has it meant to you?"

"I guess it's meant I'm attractive and that people want me," she replied thoughtfully.

"Exactly. They want you, but in your experience many have wanted you in the same way they want food or wine!"

"You're right. They wanted to use me, to consume me. And I guess—I think—maybe—I wanted to consume them too. Their adoration makes me feel worthwhile." She was more insightful than I had anticipated.

And I was amazed at the insights she herself turned up in the rest of the hour. Jonah's crass rejection of Rana, I was beginning to think, was something of a God-send after all.

She admitted that, at times, she imagined herself falling at Nachar's feet, begging his forgiveness for whatever she had done to offend him. At least she would have his attention, however much it would degrade her. In those moments of desperation, she cared little for the invisible God and His love, she allowed, for if He *really* loved her He wouldn't continually deprive her of what she wanted so much.

"There are moments," she finished, "when I realize that there must be a higher love—one that gives itself without demanding in return. I wish I could find that kind of love."

As Rana left my office that day, I could not help but draw comparisons between her and Jonah. She was preoccupied with love, and he with justice. If only the cause of each could be shared with the other! I believed Rana would learn and improve. I wasn't so sure about Jonah.

What would happen to Jonah himself at the hands of God? And the hands of Ninevites who, rumor had it, were beginning to feel Jonah had duped them with his forceful preaching. Some felt he was a charlatan, a political infiltrator come to propagandize Assyria and thus weaken its hold on Israel.

As I left for the day, I could not escape a vague, unsettling fear for him.

9

Back to His God

Come, ye faithful, raise the strain
Of triumphant gladness;
God hath bro't His Israel
Into joy from sadness.
'Tis the spring of souls today:
Christ hath burst His prison
And from three days' sleep in death
As a sun hath risen.*

The day after my visits with Rana and Jonah was, blessedly, free from appointments. Shem was going to be in town again, and he had invited me to attend a conference for psychologists at the university. I also hoped to have some chance to consult with him again to see what he might suggest by way of therapeutic maneuvers for Jonah's anger.

As it turned out, we would have no opportunity to discuss Jonah. If I'd expected a totally relaxed day, free from conflict, I was to be disappointed.

The sun was just gilding the university towers as Shem and I arrived. We were going to be a couple of minutes late for the opening lecture by Banipal, because Shem had been late. He had never, like me, placed great importance on punctuality. I became uncomfortable when I was even two minutes behind schedule, though I realized Yahweh was granting my prayer for freedom from this compulsive behavior, finding myself less ruffled when patients came late for appointments.

Nonetheless, I was aware that most heads turned, ob-

---

*John of Damascus, c. 750; tr. John M. Neale, c. 1859, alt.

serving our disruption, when we entered the auditorium five minutes into Banipal's address.

Banipal's topic made me immediately uneasy, especially in light of his recent "conversion." It was this: the need for psychologists to become more scientific and for psychology as a discipline to develop a true science of human behavior.

Banipal's lecture was more than a cold rehearsal of data. He waxed eloquent, stirring the assembly. He pleaded with us to become dedicated research scientists rather than soft-headed, crowd-serving, fee-collecting clinicians, trying to cure people without adequate knowledge of the causes and remedies for emotional illnesses.

"What," demanded Banipal, "remains for science to accomplish? We have learned to build towers to heights unprecedented in the history of the Plain of Shinar—er, regardless of a few structural flaws. We have developed the science of warfare to the point that no nation can stand in the path of Assyrian weaponry. We have charted the pathways of the stars. We have knowledge of the planets and their influence on human lives, medicines to cure human sicknesses, principles of navigation enabling trading vessels to traverse the Great Sea like a lake. We have done many marvelous things. What we have *not* done is develop the ability to accurately predict and reliably control human behavior.

"How," orated the impassioned professor, "without learning to predict and *control* behavior, can we hope to develop the utopia we all dream of bequeathing to human society? Never will we have peace unless we can change the aggressive behavior of man! There will be no true plenty, even in the midst of economic abundance, until we can engineer the greed-free human being." He paused at this point, his silence full of drama.

"And who, my friends, must bring it all to pass?" he thundered on. "Psychologists! The world waits for us to develop the necessary methods. Whose is the awesome task of altering the human being until he is fit to live in the coming new age which is mankind's true destiny? Who, if not psychologists? To us belongs the most glorious of all work, the designing and building of no less than a new human race on the rock-solid foundation of science."

His talk closed with an evangelistic ring, a call to dedicate ourselves to build a new world on top of the psychological ruins left by previous "systems."

The way he said that last word made me very uncomfortable. Shem was anxiously pinching at his lower lip and tapping his foot. Though much of the audience was on its feet at the close of Banipal's lecture, cheering and applauding, a few were not. I noticed that many side-long glances were cast our way when Shem and I stayed in our seats. Shem would not even clap.

As Banipal disappeared from the platform, Shem nudged me. "Come on. Let's go." Thinking he wanted to catch a breath of air before the next speaker, I followed him out of the auditorium. Instead of heading for the open air, however, Shem turned toward the side door, from which Banipal had just exited. There stood Banipal, I must say, with the most self-satisfied look I have seen.

I hadn't realized how coiled Shem was, how ready for a confrontation, until we approached Banipal. "Professor Banipal," he opened, his voice even, though I knew him well enough to pick up a note of annoyance, "science explains mechanisms, but not mysteries. Don't you recognize any true mysteries?"

"None that we cannot research." Banipal was a study in aplomb. "In a sense, Shem, there are mysteries. But, of course, a mystery is only a puzzle not yet solved by scientific procedures."

Though Banipal made as if to leave, Shem pursued. "Your reply means that for you a mystery is only a mechanism which science has not yet gotten around to taking apart into its component pieces."

"If you like, yes. I think there are no mysteries in the sense that there is no phenomenon which, in principle, must always remain inaccessible to science." Banipal, I could tell at once, was on familiar ground—that is, the good hard ground of materialism.

More than Banipal's words, I could read into his tone: patronizing. The almost pitying look in his eyes as he studied Shem said, "Tut, tut. Such a muddled head. What a messy clutter to speak of abstractions—mysteries."

Then I knew. Whatever had happened at his "conversion," Banipal's unrelenting rationalism, his godlike insistence on holding everything a slave to his perception and analysis, was back in control—if it had ever been crushed in the first place.

"You can explain and explain," Shem was saying. "You can take apart my brain, reducing it to cells and even to the buildingblocks of cells. But having achieved this, you will not have come one hairsbreadth closer to understanding me—a human being, made in the image of God. You must first turn me into a mechanism and then dissect the mechanism. But then, having anaylzed me, you have lost me. I have eluded you. You have your mechanism, but you don't have *me*! And I will always elude you because I belong to a realm of reality that is inaccessible to your assumptions, methods, and instruments."

Though Banipal's eyes were tense, he did not lose his decorum. "Shem, your brain is a machine. The reason it seems a mystery to you is that it is enormously complex and finely designed. Discovering all there is to know about it is a gargantuan task. But it is not insurmountable. We will know. And we will control the human brain. That's what the science of psychology is all about."

Far from being intimidated, Shem leaped on Banipal's argument. "If you are correct, and you yourself are a mere machine, then everything you are saying right now is only the clattering of a machine. You vitiate your own argument. Your nervous system works as it must and churns out the words and sentences that are its product, just as the siege-engine churns out flying boulders. Your thoughts are only mechanical events, produced at random, and cannot possibly have any necessary relation to the truth, though you suffer from the illusion that you are speaking as a free person."

Banipal winced. Shem had certainly touched one weak spot in his system of thought. If man was a mere machine, then there could be no truth, for there were no free minds to think it. There were only machines which processed whatever was put into them and spewed out the results according to the inexorable laws of their design.

"You are now implying some sort of freedom for the human person," Banipal said, with a tone-like disgust, as if Shem had just introduced obscene material into the discussion. "It is quite obvious to me that, if we want a science of psychology, we must have the faith to believe in the ultimate lawfulness of human behavior. You must, Shem. You cannot expect psychology to proceed ahead, to make real gains, unless you acknowledge that there can be no freedom. If we are really free, our behavior is unpredictable and there goes your science!"

"Banipal, if you can become so 'religious' as to speak of faith in the ultimate predictability of behavior, it seems to me you could come just as well to speak of faith in God."

"Except, my young friend, I have tried that. Other than some sentimental feelings, there is no evidence for your God-hypothesis. No evidence at all. Meanwhile, there is abundant evidence that the faith-in-science hypothesis pays rich dividends. Look what it has done for mankind already, all because a few pioneers could say, 'I have faith that science will come to know how to do this.' "

Shem was not to be deterred. "Let me tell you some things you will never discover by the methods of science, Professor Banipal. Let's start with your premise that a science of psychology is extremely valuable and important. Why is it so valuable? How do you know that prediction and control of behavior are truly worthwhile? You will say to me that such a science can bring to man the things all men truly desire. I doubt that you are correct about what men desire. But granting that you know what all men want, how do you know that it is good and valuable to bring about what men want? Men have often wanted things which turned out *not* to be good for them.

"You will say," Shem continued, as Banipal tried to object, "that *you* know what is good for people. And if that is not acceptable, you'll suggest that a panel of wise men—psychologists, of course, and ethicists, and philosophers, and perhaps a judge or two—might be designed to determine what good changes we should make in men with our science. And you will repress a thought which ought to occur to you, because it is true—namely, that panels of the wisest men have often made tragic decisions for others in the history of our race. How can you believe that any group of men will know and do what is good? Can't you see that the decision-makers' own interests will most likely determine what is 'good' for all the rest?"

Banipal did not reply, so Shem continued, "I will ask you some questions you will never answer through scientific investigation, Professor.

"Why are we here?—and why is the world here? You'll say that such questions are meaningless. But don't you see that your labeling everything science cannot comment upon as 'meaningless' is purely arbitrary?—another item on your list of assumptions? Haven't you noticed that, if you don't know why you are on the earth, you have no real reason to do anything? You occupy yourself with science. Why? If you have no idea why you are here, or for that matter, why the universe is here, what gives you the right to trouble your experimental animals to run mazes rather than run free in the back alleys and garbage dumps they love? How can you be sure you are doing what is right?"

Part of me was almost embarrassed by Shem's forcefulness. But I remained rooted and silent as he drove onward.

"Can you explain love? I don't mean the kind of love Nachar chatters about. Such 'love' amounts to no more than using others to satisfy desires. I speak of a love that dies for the beloved. Such love, seeing need in another, depletes self to meet that need. Not self-actualizing love, but self-sacrificing love."

Banipal did not lose his composure, though to my own way of thinking my friend's arguments amounted to the professor's undoing. "Shem," he replied, "science can, in principle, explain *everything*." Midthought, he stopped, glancing distractedly at the nearby street. "You know, I just remembered it's my daughter's birthday. I did so want to bring home a plaything for her. Would you mind if we continued this most interesting discussion another time? I really must go."

Shem, perhaps because he was now winded, said very little on the way back to my office. As we walked, I found myself thinking about Jonah and how he would have reacted to Banipal in such an encounter. To his ears, I was certain, Banipal's beliefs would amount to foolishess. *To be angry with God, I reflected, is to know Him passionately. Therefore, wretched and miserable as he is, Jonah is better off than the smug, self-satisfied Banipal who loves his child, chooses to trust in psychology, then promptly forgets what his own existence taught him. Then he proceeds to persuade others that he is only a machine.*

Back at my office, I brewed some coffee and, finally, broke the ruminating silence that had fallen between us.

"I had never thought of how imperfectly such devotees as Banipal serve their empirical idol until just now," I began. "You made a telling point. I wonder if he will bury what you said to him? Or if he'll wonder about the answers to your questions?

"And, by the way," I added, "Banipal isn't the only one of Nineveh's erstwhile penitents who has returned to his old ways. Nachar is carrying his teaching into the bedroom again. I just accepted as a patient a young woman who threw herself into the river after one of his 'teaching sessions.' "

"She probably asked for it!" Shem replied callously.

"Just because Nachar doesn't talk like Banipal, it doesn't mean he thinks as you do, Shem," I replied. "You can't possibly believe he is maintaining these righteous-sounding values while he feeds his lusts with the bodies of naive young students.

"At any rate, this young woman shared your view of Nachar's wisdom—to the point where she became angry enough with herself to die by her own doing."

"What have you been doing to treat her?" he asked, politely, I thought, but not deeply interested.

"I'm trying to help her see the incident as a sin, but no more than that, and to know that God will forgive her if she is penitent. She insists that it is Nachar she wants to forgive her. She cannot believe that he has any faults."

Suddenly, I saw patterns I had not noticed before, and I kept talking to let these new ideas take shape. "I see now some of what Yahweh must suffer. I've always been so attentive to the suffering of my patients! I've never before noticed that God must finally bear it *all*.

"When their idols betray them, people become angry with God. Jonah, for instance, refuses to allow God to be righteous in all that He does. Jonah has an idol, and its name is retribution. He exonerates his idol, insisting that it can do no wrong, even at the cost of accusing Yahweh. Perhaps Banipal is also angry at God for reserving mysteries to himself to which Banipal is not a party. Banipal, too, is blind to the sins of his idol, science. Do we all shift our conflicts onto the back of God and resolve them by blaming Him for the failures of our idols? Do we all struggle to defend our idols against the God of truth?"

"Perhaps we do," Shem answered softly. "Perhaps we do."

10

Changes

Our hearts be pure from evil
That we may see aright
The Lord in rays eternal
Of resurrection light
And, list'ning to his accents,
May hear so calm and plain,
His own "All hail!" and, hearing,
May raise the victor strain. *

"Well, forty days have come and gone, and Nineveh stands as strong as ever!" Jonah rasped his opening line at our next session. This time, his normally-darting eyes were flat.

He paused, and I waited for him to come to what was really on his mind. I perked my ears, for I thought I heard in his tone a crucial, yet potentially dangerous shift from anger to a new emotional state.

Evidently, he was continuing to insist that his notion of justice should govern reality—even at the cost of denying God the right to do what He wished with His own, even at great cost to his own human soul.

I didn't expect that Jonah, with his spiritual roots in the Hebrew tradition, would opt for self-destruction. But you couldn't be too careful. There had been instances.

"Have you ever thought about hurting yourself, taking your own life?" I asked.

Jonah laughed bitterly. "No way! I don't have any hope

---

*John of Damascus, c. 750; tr. John M. Neale, 1863, alt.

97

for *this* world—but I don't want to destroy my chances for confronting God in the next. I want to stand before Yahweh and ask Him, 'Why have you dealt with me thus?' If I were to take my own life, I might spend the ages to come in the prison house of the dead. How could I stand before my Persecutor then?

"Of course, I may be doomed to the darkness of Sheol anyway. Yahweh has removed himself far from me. I have always been a poor sleeper, but during these weeks, I can't sleep a wink. So I cry to Him, but He doesn't hear or answer. 'How long?' I ask Him. 'How long will you continue to hide your face from me?' But there is no answer for me in all the empty heavens."

I was reassured that he would not take his own life, but my heart ached nonetheless.

"The nights *are* the worst part," he continued. "The shadows mock me. My hut is falling down. It doesn't keep the night wind and rain away. I have no will to cut branches to repair it. It only reminds me that I'm a failure."

"What do you mean, Jonah?"

"I have prophesied and it has not come to pass. Moses says that such a prophet is not a true prophet. I shouldn't have preached to Nineveh. All the while, I knew. I *knew* that terrible mercy. If only there were such mercy for me! But I've betrayed my country by rescuing her deadly enemy. If I hadn't come, Nineveh would now be a heap of ashes, and Israel would be free. My own nation won't even have mercy on me now. I can't even go home to die."

"You are a failure because Nineveh *wasn't* destroyed?"

"Of course. I predicted it, didn't I?"

"What, exactly, did you preach in the streets of Nineveh?"

" 'Yet forty days and Nineveh will be destroyed,' I proclaimed. I said it because I was told to say it. But I knew that Yahweh's terrible mercy could invalidate my words. He is so quick to forgive, especially the ignorant! Evidently, it isn't so easy for Him to have mercy on one like me!"

"Why can't God forgive you, Jonah?"

"Because of the enormity of my failures. I ran from Him because I knew of that mercy. Then, from fear of Him, I did His bidding. I should have refused to preach, no matter what He did. But I preached. And I prophesied something which didn't come to pass. I hated Him because He failed me. But now I know that it is against me that all this must be counted, and such failure can't be forgiven." Jonah's despair was total.

"You are saying your failures are so huge, so sinful, it's impossible for God to forgive them?"

"Maybe. He refuses to answer when I call to Him. He turns His face away. Why else, unless it's because of my failures?"

"Why else? Good question, Jonah," I replied. "Why don't you answer it? Give me a few possible reasons."

"He can't abide me, that's the reason."

I pressed him. "Just because you can't abide yourself doesn't automatically imply that God feels as you do."

"He has agreed with me in very little else," said Jonah, "so I suppose there's no harm in speculating that once again His reasons and mine are as far from one another as east is from west."

"Then do it. Tell me, what other conceivable causes are there for your feeling that God doesn't listen or speak to you?"

"Well, He could be letting me feel alienated from Him to allow me a taste of what I wanted when I took ship to Tarshish," Jonah mused.

I interjected: "Like a father saying to his child, 'The stove is hot and it will burn you, but if you must find out for yourself, go ahead. Touch only lightly and you'll see for yourself.' In that case, He would be dealing with you in His great mercy."

"Yes, I suppose," Jonah replied, reluctantly though.

"What else might God be up to, Jonah?"

"Simply waiting—waiting for me to do something. He could be doing that," he mumbled, barely audible.

I also waited. Nearly in a whisper, he continued.

"He could be putting the squeeze on me again. It appears that I respond when I receive hard treatment, doesn't it? He had me cast into the sea, swallowed by some slimey thing and spit out as a lump of vomit. Then I did what He commanded. Perhaps now His right arm is bared against me."

"Perhaps. With what in view?" I had an idea.

"I don't know. He hasn't commanded me to do anything that I know of."

"Perhaps He is waiting for you to forgive Him," I suggested.

The quiet mood shattered in a roar. "What *right* does mortal man have to speak of *forgiving God*, the all-righteous One? It's ridiculous—presumptous even to think such thoughts."

But the truth also came out. "Mostly, I don't *want* to forgive Him. If only I could get Him to back down somehow and admit I'm right!"

"But, Jonah," I braved, "how can anger be cured except by forgiveness?"

"You're going in circles," he accused. "You keep telling me to do what I can't do. How can I turn from my principles, from justice—from right itself—and act as though none of it mattered? Perhaps you could do it. You psychologists have no principles. The claim to justice is all I have. All I live for. Even Yahweh can't take that from me!"

The session was over, and I stood up. As I opened the office door, Jonah stood too, and plaintively asked, "Are we getting anywhere?"

I recognized the ploy which I had seen countless times before. It was an effort to prolong the session rather than go out into the aching void of seemingly endless depression.

I sympathized, but I knew I could not let him bind me. If I said we were making progress, Jonah would most likely call me a liar because of the ache of his depression. If I said we were not progressing, he would most likely quit the therapy. Mostly, I recognized the ploy as an attempt to draw me into a prolonged conversation after the therapeutic hour was over.

All I could do was hand him the truth: "Are we getting anywhere? That, Jonah, is something you know better than I. You are the one who lives inside your skin. I'll see you next session."

As he passed by me, the thought came unbidden that I might never see Jonah again.

11

Celebration

"Welcome, happy morning!"
Age to age shall say;
"Hell today is vanquished,
Heav'n is won today!"
Lo, the Dead is living.
God forevermore!
Him, their true Creator,
*All His works adore.**

The next morning, Saturday, I woke suddenly, as if some-one had shaken me awake. The morning was dim-lit, still but for the singing of birds. Suddenly, and with all the brilliance of a resurrection, the morning light flashed over the hills east of Nineveh. Perhaps the day felt especially inviting to me because I was planning a picnic with my family.

As Miriam fussed with the picnic basket, ten-year-old Leah offered her always-inventive suggestions. "Mom, why not put the dates inside the loaf of bread? I just know it would be delicious!" And, "Can I put some berry juice in the milk, Mom? Please?" Leah was unfailingly creative and had a pen-chant for improving things.

Outside, our twelve-year-old, Avnor, was throwing his knife at a target I had mounted for him. "Son," I called to him, "will you please put the bathing clothes and towels in the basket? Oh, and the blanket, too."

---

*Salve, festa, dies, Venantius Fortunatus, c. 590, cento; tr. John Ellerton, 1868, alt.

"Sure, Dad," he answered. He was always at his best when he was about to go on an outing. "Can I bring a ball?"

"Absolutely, Son."

Our family had discovered a picnic spot that most people only dream about. It was on the riverbank at the edge of a farm, about a mile beyond the city wall. We always obtained the farmer's permission to picnic on his land, and he invariably consented graciously. Others, we knew, had been rebuffed by him. We were favored, I think, because Miriam's mother had gone to school with his wife. Perhaps, in his mind, that made us trustworthy.

Here, the Tigris widened and slowed. There were no treacherous currents or sudden drop-offs. It was here that Miriam had taught both Av and Leah to swim. Along the bank were willow trees, their boughs bending to the ground like the arms of the Father reaching down from heaven to touch His children. The ground was carpeted with rich green grass, dappled yellow and gold with mustard flowers and poppies.

After the brisk hike out from Nineveh, and a game of catch with Avnor, the four of us lay on a bed of grass and flowers, drowsy in the hot noon sun. I felt the week's tensions taking their reluctant leave of the muscles in my shoulders and back.

How good it is, I thought sleepily, *to be sons and daughters of the King!* It was then I heard strange voices, somewhere down river from where we lay. *The farmer, or his sons*, I thought absently, and paid no more attention.

As the sun climbed higher in the sky, the water felt cool and refreshing. After we had had enough swimming, we spread our picnic lunch in the shade of a large willow. Av ran to the farmer's well and pulled up our skin of berry-flavored milk, now icy cold from the chill of the deep, underground spring waters in which we had immersed it for several hours. Miriam had unwrapped loaves of crunchy, dark bread and chunks of creamy, white cheese. Taken together with a salad of lettuce, green onions, and cucumbers, and topped off with sweet summer fruits, it was a feast fit for a celebration on this glorious day.

After lunch, the children ran off to explore on their own, leaving Miriam and me to ourselves. Again, I stretched out on my back in the shade, while Miriam lay next to me with her head on my arm. It was a time to talk.

I rarely discussed my patients with anyone, even my wife. Confidentiality was something I owed them, and it was important to most people that the information they gave me in confidence be kept strictly to myself. On the other hand, I had often spoken to Miriam about Jonah during the past weeks. I did not regard this as a violation of confidence, since by now there was no one in Nineveh who did not know something of the story of Jonah.

I could not, even on this festal day, put Jonah and his extraordinary experiences far from my consciousness.

"Frankly, I'm stumped," I admitted, chewing lazily on a blade of grass. "Most of Nineveh is turning its back on Jonah now. But why did they listen to him in the first place? It's a pretty hard thing to swallow when some blotchy-looking guy in a ragged tunic shouts at you, 'Repent, or die!' "

"I know what you mean," Miriam replied, sitting up suddenly. "It was crude. Harsh. Unsophisticated. The sort of thing prophets and pseudo-prophets have been shouting at people since the beginning of time, it seems. I've been wondering why anyone would pay attention to him, too."

I added. "What he said was no different than the usual threats of the right-wing, religious fanatics. People are accustomed to brushing off his kind with a chuckle. And he preached with such hatred and anger, it's a wonder Jonah wasn't skinned and dismembered or beaten to death on the spot!"

"It should have made people either furious or amused," Miriam replied. "Instead it made them afraid. Now that Nineveh has been spared, I wonder what will happen to that fear?"

That was a question I had not considered. What does happen to fear when it ripens? Nor was I about to ponder the subject much deeper on so lilting an afternoon, with a delightful breeze stirring the grass.

The breeze brought us a shimmer of voices, and I thought of Av and Leah. "What do you suppose the children are doing? We haven't seen them for quite a while."

"I'm sure they're all right," Miriam replied. "But maybe we should take a walk and look for them." She jumped up playfully. "Catch me, if you can!"

I leaped to my feet and pursued her. When I caught her, we kissed. Then hand-in-hand, we strolled along the river.

Soon we found Leah fishing from the bank. Inventive as she was, she had made a fishhook from a little bronze hairpin she had been wearing, and had baited it with a piece of cheese from the lunchbox. With her improvised tackle, she had managed to land a small carp. Av had found a tree to climb, and was playing ship's lookout.

From there, we set off on the high path, an old animal trail along the bluffs above the riverbank, which made it possible to view ever-changing riverscapes of lush beauty.

We had not gone far when we heard men's voices, faint at first and growing louder as we approached. In a few moments, we found ourselves directly above the speakers. We could not see them, nor could they see us, since they were evidently in a hollow place beneath the bluff where we were walking. Their coarse chatter made it obvious that they were in the process of becoming very drunk. We could not help overhearing a conversation. To our utter astonishment, they were discussing Jonah!

Drawn by this unusual coincidence—was it coincidence?—we sat down softly, certain the speakers had no more idea we were there than we had had forewarning of their presence.

"I tell ya, I wanna be there when the prophet gets what's

comin' to 'im!" said a rumbly, low voice.

"Ye're right. It's not gonna be good fer 'im, seein' 's how he done what he done to us traders."

"Tiglon had a fine li'l bi'ness goin', an' we was all gettin' rich. Then this bird come along an'—whoosh! There goes Tiglon, right down on his knees. An' tha's the end of the slave trade in Nineveh."

Miriam opened her mouth to whisper something to me. I put my finger to my lips to stop her. This was too important to miss. We had heard about Tiglon's "conversion" and the fact that he had freed all of his slaves. It had awed us when we first heard about it, because Tiglon had always been one of the most evil men in the city. A former career soldier, he was infamous for the exotic tortures he had dreamed up for foreign prisoners. Some had even committed suicide, rather than die slowly in agony, for his amusement. If he was throwing off the sackcloth, then Jonah . . . I strained my ear.

The wheezy one was still speaking. "Why don't Tiglon jes' start up ag'in where he lef' off when he repented of his sins? Hahaha, Hehehe."

The two dissolved into gails of laughter and wheezing, evidently at the notion of Tiglon actually repenting of his sins. When they recovered, the rumbly-sounding drunk replied, "Tiglon, he'd like to get them sins back now! He's repentin' about repentin' in the first place."

More wild laughter. Then: "Why don't we start up sellin' slaves ag'in?" asked the wheezy one.

"Cuz Tiglon can't git the merchandise anymore. The army officer who used to bring them pris'ners of war to us says we can't have any more. He's mad about Tiglon repentin' and cuttin' off his best outlet. He's sellin' pris'ners to other parts of the empire now. Says he ain't never gonna trust Tiglon no more."

"What's Tiglon gonna do?"

"I dunno," came the rumbly reply. "He's talkin' about gittin' the prophet. I figure he'll kill 'im. Tiglon's good at killin'. 'Member the customer what took four prime Ethiopian slaves an' wouldn' pay his bill? Tiglon had his arms and legs tore off. He died of bleedin'." The man slurred the last sentence with mock solemnity.

"Then, ag'in, th' law's been crackin' down hard on murder lately. Order of the emperor hisself. Tiglon always knows just what he can git away with," wheezed his friend.

"You're right there. Maybe Tiglon'll only hurt 'im. Anyhow, I wouldn' wanna be Jonah, not fer all the monkeys in Tarshish! Gimme that bottle, will ya?"

There was silence, and I could imagine the two sots taking a long pull on the wine bottle. Miriam and I exchanged glances which meant, "Let's go."

Softly, though we were not in immediate danger from the two stupefied slave traders, we gathered our children and our picnic gear and walked back to town. The men had not seen us, I was sure. If they had, we might be in danger too.

Though the children were still in a light mood, I was silent all the way home. For her part, Miriam looked disappointed that the day had been ruined for me by this unfortunate happenstance.

And inwardly, I wrestled with myself. Was I getting carried away to pay attention to the babbling of two winos? Perhaps I was losing my sense of perspective being around Jonah's paranoia. People don't go around killing each other for preaching. On the other hand, Tiglon had been vicious before . . . before Jonah had put the fear of God into him. Suddenly Miriam's question came back to me: *Now that Nineveh has been spared, I wonder what will happen to that fear?*

What indeed? I mused, half to myself, half in prayer, as we neared home again. From the heavens, surrounding the westering sun that lighted our way with red-gold brilliance, there was only silence.

12

I Cannot Tell What This Love May Be Which Cometh to All But Not to Me

O wondrous love, whose depth no heart hath sounded,
That brought Thee here, by foes and thieves surrounded!
All worldly pleasure, heedless, I was trying
*While Thou wert dying.**

The slurred voices of those two drunks were never far from the surface of my thoughts in the coming days. With my other patients, I had to fight to keep my mind off Jonah and the strange mixture of love and justice with which Yahweh had dealt with the prophet.

And during my times with Rana, it was impossible not to make connections and comparisons. The love she had received from her father cared nothing for justice. He had always given, and given generously.

"Anything I wanted, he gave me," she mused during our session the very next week. "He loved me so, he couldn't bear to deny me anything. I once wished for a pony. The next

---

Herzliebster Jesu, Johann Heermann, 1630; tr. Catherine Winkworth, 1863, alt.

morning, a beautiful bay stood tethered to our back fence. Daddy would send someone to school with my lunch at exactly 12 o'clock so my food would be hot, though everyone else ate cold sandwiches. If I got tired of my clothes, new dresses appeared—even if I hadn't outgrown the old ones. I don't remember being refused anything—ever.

"Daddy was so kind and good! One time—I think I was about fifteen—I had a little too much wine at a party, and when I came home my mother insisted on making a scene. She said I was 'drunk'! She wanted so much for Daddy to punish me. But he understood kids. And, besides, he just couldn't take hassles! He wanted his home to be a place of peace and harmony. Though Mother wanted him to punish me, he just took me aside and had a talk with me. He didn't want me to feel bad about myself." She smiled at the memory of her father's tenderness.

The father Rana described—his unwillingness to discipline—I had heard it all before. How very little those parental talks accomplish! I had seen too many children whose parents substituted talk for action. Little did these adults suspect that such "talks" were actually rewarding to their children. In the final analysis, they promoted bad behavior because, for the child, they offered a good deal of reinforcing parental attention.

"Did your father ever insist on your keeping the rules, Rana?" I asked, trying not to reveal my irritation at such indulgence.

"Oh, yes. Daddy wanted me to be good. But he understood when I couldn't do everything perfectly. For instance, there were times when I couldn't get the dishes done, right? My homework and my boyfriend and school and everything would keep me too busy. Mom would yell, of course. But Daddy understood. He would tell her that I couldn't be expected to act like an adult. And that was true. I was only a child. You understand, don't you?" Her eyes practically offered me a bribe to agree with her.

I decided to ignore the demand in her eyes and voice, to offer her no support for her erroneous expectations. "Your father always got you off the hook," I summarized.

"Well—" She evidently didn't like my way of putting it. "He had a way of making things turn out all right. I can't explain it any better than that."

Without any further thought, she plunged into another story: Her parents told her once that she could have a new coat as a reward for keeping her room clean for three weeks. She did not clean her room, but she did get the coat. Once again, in her view, Daddy had been "understanding."

By now, I could tell that this sort of thing implanted in her the belief that true love knew nothing about justice. And that justice, when it appeared on the scene, meant that others were "unreasonable" and not "understanding."

For Rana, justice had become love's antagonist.

She also learned to see herself as a child, and she came to believe that whoever really loved her would, accordingly, make no demands on her.

What, I thought, as she again waxed eloquent about her adoring father, *is the worth of love from one whose only aim is harmony? And what is a love that asks for nothing? Does such a love really offer the world free of charge?*

The sad thing was this: Rana had emerged from this "loving" childhood with an impoverished picture of herself. For the message communicated by her father's love was that she was valuable, yes, but only as a pretty little thing, an object of affection, to be cuddled and coddled, and never, never expected to function like a responsible adult.

Moreover, she had grown up to believe, without giving it a second thought, that anyone else who wanted to love her ought to give in the same way. Even more, Rana believed at a deep level that, without a constant supply of such love, she could not live.

"You thought you had found an even higher love in the teachings of Nachar, didn't you, Rana?" I asked, when she again fell silent.

"Oh, yes. He spoke to my heart. And what he said seemed so new, so—so alive with a love that would fulfill my deepest yearnings! I wanted to experience that love."

"Do you suppose that in Nachar you thought you had found a man who offered something like the love your father had given you?"

She paused to stare at me with wide eyes. Then she looked away. "I wonder. I wonder if that's what I've been looking for all my life. Professor Nachar was so different from other men. I had not known anyone like him." Her gaze had settled on the window. She turned to face me once again. "Can I tell you about my boyfriend in Babylon?"

"By all means. Was he a 'giving' person, too?"

"I thought he was. I believed Ven adored me. He seemed to worship me. In fact, he called me his 'goddess.' He told me again and again how beautiful I was. He said he'd do anything for me. And he gave all this love freely, demanding nothing in return. At least that's how it appeared at first."

She hesitated, almost embarrassed, then went on. "After a while I began to feel uncomfortable around Ven. He never came right out and asked for anything. But he began to withdraw. He would hardly talk to me. I finally realized he was sulking. When I begged him to tell me what was wrong, he insisted it was nothing. At last, without telling me directly, he let me know he was feeling deprived, and that I had not been giving him my total attention, which he had come to believe he needed to live."

"What made him feel that way?" I probed.

"Oh, little things. Most people wouldn't pay any attention to them. Like my talking to another guy, for instance. Not at length, just a sentence or two. That was all it took to make Ven clam up. Then I would feel guilty and confused, wondering what I had done to hurt him."

"You were an easy mark for such tactics," I remarked. "Hadn't you learned, at your mother's knee, to please others out of guilt?"

"You mean my mother used guilt to make me obey her?" Rana asked.

"What you've told me before sounds that way. Wouldn't you rather have been trained with clearly specified and regularly applied consequences than with those ugly feelings of incomprehensible guilt?" I inquired.

Rana considered this for a moment, her eyes closed. "I never thought of it like that," she finally replied. "I always took it for granted that punishment was something awful and that only parents who didn't really love their children hurt them. I always believed I was loved into being good, without any punishment. . . . But I see now I wasn't. No, it wasn't that way at all! I was punished, wasn't I? The punishment was those horrid feelings of being bad and wrong. I never understood why I felt them. I only realized that they returned whenever I was around Mother. And I feel them today whenever I go home."

Things were falling into place for Rana. I let her go at her own pace. How often, as a novice counselor, I had spoiled a patient's efforts by chiming in with "interpretations" right and left instead of letting the person discover truth.

"So, in a sense, Ven was like both of my parents rolled into one person," she said, with dawning insight. "Like my father, he made me believe I was a perfect, innocent child who could do no wrong. But, like my mother, Ven made me feel bad whenever I didn't do what he wanted me to." There was a sense of wonder in her voice as the past came clear to her.

"I began to want to get away. But the more I tried to escape from Ven, the more he surrounded me with his clinging love. I believed I needed his devotion too desperately to do without it. I thought I couldn't bear the self-loathing his hurt silence aroused in me whenever I even hinted at breaking free.

"You know," she paused, "I think I came to Nineveh partly to get away from Ven, partly to escape from my parents. All three of them loved me. But their love hurt, and I didn't understand why. I thought it was because of something that was wrong with me.

"Maybe all this explains why I was so thrilled when I heard Professor Nachar lecture about love. He described something I had always dreamed of: a love so unselfish that when two people were spiritually united in this uplifting bond, they would lose the boundaries that divided them into separate selves, and merge into a self-annihilating oneness."

"With neither lover having to give or suffer anything?" I asked.

She shook her head. "There was no talk of giving or suffering. And I thought, how perfect such a love would be—a love that would transform life and cost nothing, a love without the awful guilt I had felt about Ven."

I wanted her to explore Nachar's behavior. Actually, I wanted to put a hole in his drum for good. "You found Nachar's love was not as you had anticipated?"

The tears were coming. Rana's lips trembled, but she did not speak.

"What is love, Rana?" I asked gently.

"Caring for someone, I suppose," she began slowly. "Giving them yourself, and trying to do what they want you to do." Clearly, she had never really analyzed what she meant by the word which had so occupied her thoughts and fantasies.

"Trying to do whatever they want you to do?" I repeated the salient part of her definition.

"If you can, yes," she said. "If you love someone, you care for them enough to give them what they want."

"Anything they want?"

"Of course! Love doesn't hold anything back!"

"What if the beloved should become despondent and ask you for something lethal with which to destroy himself?" I suggested. "Is it loving to give him what he wants then?"

"Oh no! Of course not. You wouldn't give poison to someone you love, even if they begged you for it," Rana replied.

"Then you have to change your definition of love, don't you, Rana?"

"I guess so. I'd have to say that love is not giving another person whatever he wants, but only what isn't harmful to him."

"Or what is *good* for him?"

"Yes, love is giving another person things that are good for him and not things that will harm him," she answered.

She was on the verge of breakthrough. I continued. "And would you agree that giving another person whatever he wants could very easily be unloving, though it might at first appear to be loving both to the lover and the beloved?"

"Yes, I see that. I see it now." The tears were flowing freely—freeing tears. "What I always thought was love might not have been so very loving. When Daddy gave me everything I wanted, when Ven told me only what I wanted to hear, when my parents couldn't bring themselves to punish me for doing wrong, it might not have been love at all. It might have been their own needs they were meeting all along. Real love might even hurt me sometimes, right?"

What happened inside me when Rana uttered those words was like twin bolts of lightning crossing. For the first time, I saw that Rana and Jonah were exact opposites, though both were struggling against distorted ideas about love.

Jonah had yet to discover the merciful love of Yahweh. Thus far, he had room in his heart only for meticulous and untempered justice. He who had never learned to accept love had to come into the joy of it. Conversely, Rana had to know the love of Yahweh as justice, for she had received, in the guise of love, only soft, indulgent ardor which cared nothing for justice. Overprizing the love that consumes, she must esteem instead the love that gives.

With Rana's just-stirring awareness, I knew she was on the verge of finding what she sought: Perfect love. There was so much I had to tell her, about a love which never exploits, but always acts for the good of the other; that disciplines, sometimes with hard lessons, and it even tolerates the anger of the beloved without quailing; that delights in the beloved more than Rana's father delighted in his charming daughter, for it seeks, not a plaything but fellowship. In giving it is fulfilled, and in blessing it is blessed.

"Rana, there is Someone I must tell you about," I began. First, I knew she would have to forgive Him. He waited to forgive her.

13

I Gave My Back to the Smiters

O sacred Head, now wounded,
  With grief and shame weighed down;
Now scornfully surrounded
  With thorns, Thine only crown.
O sacred Head, what glory,
  What bliss till now was Thine!
Yet, tho' despised and gory,
  I joy to call Thee mine.*

The following week was one of high humidity and thunder storms. On the day of Jonah's next appointment, I kept nervously checking the hour. Perhaps it was the sultry air, the gray cloud covering that drooped low overhead. I was sweating profusely, even with my office windows open—the lifeless air left even the draperies limp.

And all the time I felt—I did not know why—that a dread thing was about to break over us all.

Something was not as it should be. Was it only the oppressive heat and humidity? The threatening storm? Inside, I heard again whispers I'd picked up in the marketplace, and the raucous, violent voices of Tiglon's two drunken men.

I shook myself, took a deep breath and again checked the hour. It was nearly time for Jonah to come. I was pleased

---

**O Haupt voll Blut und Wunden*, Based on the Latin; Bernard of Clairvaux, 1153, asc.; Paul Gerhardt, 1656; Tr. composite.

with the changes I had been seeing. Although my huge patient *had* become depressed, to me that meant he was moving from his impossible locked-in position of war upon all creation and its Creator. Blaming may protect you from facing the pain of reality for a while, but the result is expensive. Finally, reality plummets down upon you, even if you have managed to continue blaming to the end. Now that Jonah had become depressed, he went right on looking for someone to blame for his difficulties. Only now he was blaming himself instead of God, and as a result he now felt worthless, desperate, and despairing. Melancholy had largely replaced Jonah's energetic fury. No man can live so alienated an existence and thrive.

Jonah would, in time, have to take the next step: he would have to move from depression and self-blame to acceptance of reality as it is. Should he choose to do so, my difficult patient might now, with the aid of the Spirit of God, become healthy.

But I did worry some about Jonah. He might choose against wholeness. What is the mysterious X-factor which causes one patient to choose to be healed and another to die? Doctors regularly confront a mystery here. One patient has the same diagnosis and the same statistical prognosis as another; both may follow the same regime of therapy and medication; but one of them progresses and gains his health, while the other remains bonded to illness. Why? What mysterious, hidden quality makes the difference? Would Jonah give up his alienation and move toward health?

My thoughts were so taken up with the prophet's crisis, I did not notice I had gotten out of my chair and begun to pace up and down, glancing regularly from my window to the street. There was no sign of Jonah; I grew anxious.

By now the top of Jonah's appointment hour had passed. It was unheard of for this compulsive client to be late or to forget a session. Of course, Jonah might have been angry with me. I tried to recall our last session. Had I done anything he could have interpreted as inimical? I had been particularly careful not to unduly hook into his paranoid notions of persecution, but I realized that I could do little to prevent his forming the belief that I was his enemy, out to get him. I began to feel the familiar knots being tied in my stomach.

As my concern increased, I had the uncomfortable feeling that I should have told Jonah what Miriam and I had overheard that day by the river.

The minutes ticked by. Ten. Twenty. No sign of him. I wiped the perspiration from my face. What should I do? *Do?* Didn't I usually relax when patients were late, realizing that there was nothing I *could* do? They would come sooner or later, and I would help them to discover the unconscious reasons for their tardiness? Why couldn't I believe it when I told myself that Jonah would arrive, eventually, or make another appointment?

If only it would rain, I thought. Perhaps if the air would clear, I would feel less anxious about him. At that moment, a burst of lightning, followed instantly by the loudest thunderclap I had ever heard, shook the Nineveh Professional Building to its foundations. I think I cried out, involuntarily, with the shock of fear that surged through me.

Thirty minutes had past. What was wrong with me? In a moment, Jonah would arrive, and I'd learn what he was trying to communicate with his tardiness. And then I heard footsteps approaching rapidly in the hall outside my office. I felt a surge of relief.

The door opened. There stood not Jonah but Shem. He was breathing heavily.

"I just came from the Waterfront Coffee Shop," he gasped. "The talk I overheard made me run straight to your office. I thought you should know. They're saying Tiglon has gone out to Jonah's hut. He's been talking revenge to whoever will listen. They say he went out there with a bunch of drunken malcontents he found hanging around the riverfront, just looking for trouble."

"Come on, Shem," I blurted. "We've got to find Jonah. His life may be in danger."

"Wait a minute!" Shem objected. "What can you do against Tiglon and his mob?"

"There's no time to explain all this to anyone else. Jonah could already be dead. We've got to hurry. Every second counts!"

With Shem at my heels, I dashed to the waiting room, yanked my raincoat off the rack, and pulled it on. As I reached for the outer door, my eye caught sight of Rana. How long had she been waiting? Obsessed with fears for Jonah, I had forgotten her!

"Oh, Rana," I stopped to apologize, "I'm so sorry. I simply must leave. It's an emergency. It's the prophet. We think he may be in danger. I can't explain now. Could you please come back tomorrow?"

"Jonah is in trouble? What's going on? I want to know!" she demanded.

"Rana, every second counts. I really can't explain, but I'm frightened. Please come back tomorrow!"

Rana stood up and reached for her coat. "I'm going with you," she said calmly.

The last thing I wanted was responsibility for Rana's safety. "You can't go!" I shot back. "Someone could get hurt. I don't know what to expect and I don't want you involved!"

She squared her shoulders, pulled herself up to her full height. "If someone is in trouble, I'm coming with you whether you like it or not."

I felt my insides rolling. But how could I stop her? Still, she had no call to endanger her life—or had she? Whether or not, it was not a time to debate.

Turning from her, I rushed out the door, down the stairs, and into the driving storm, a reluctant Shem and a stubborn Rana following close behind me.

14

You Shall Go Out in Joy

Christ Jesus lay in death's strong bands,
For our offenses given;
But now at God's right hand He stands
And brings us life from heaven;
Therefore let us joyful be
And sing to God right thankfully
Loud songs of hallelujah. Hallelujah!*

The rain pelted us, and the going was difficult as we made our way east, toward the outskirts of the great city. Along Bel Street, few shops were still open. The drinking establishments were not yet filled to capacity again, since Jonah's preaching had wellnigh emptied them. But a good part of their old trade had returned. They had enough business to remain open. I thought about how delighted many of these barkeepers would be if someone should expose Jonah's skull to the view of the entire city.

Shem, at my side, was still trying to persuade me to go to others for help. Our pace, however, made it difficult for him to say very much, and I was determined to go to my patient. Rana didn't speak. Our pace kept her breathless, but she wore a look of grim determination. For my part, I knew now I would not rest until I again heard the gravel-crusher

---

*Christ lag in Iodesbanden, Martin Luther, 1524, cento; Tr., Richard Massie, 1854, alt.

voice. Haste was imperative—perhaps we were already too late. There was truly no time to enlist the aid of anyone else. And though Jonah himself would perhaps be glad to meet death without further adieu, I truly believed that Yahweh loved His resentful son. I knew that much could yet be accomplished in Jonah. Would we arrive in time? We were two men and a woman against—I didn't know how to finish the thought!

I couldn't conceive of even a rudimentary plan. What would happen if we actually encountered the thugs? They might find it quite agreeable to kill us, too. Did I have any right to be dragging Shem into this? Should I have taken more time, made more effort to stop Rana? There would be nothing we could do against a force which so outnumbered us. I was certain that, if such a confrontation should take place, Shem and I had no chance of winning it. Nor should I expect much help from Rana.

I seemed, strangely, to be more concerned about whether I would have the courage to face death than about dying itself. I thought about what would become of my wife, my children, and my patients. Who would care for them? Would death be very painful? Perhaps they would not want to kill us. They might be content to merely beat or mutilate us. Even the thought of suffering such pain filled me with self-doubt. I did not believe even while I raced onward, that I could handle it with courage.

Our breathlessness prevented us from sharing such thoughts with each other, so we remained silent as we ran on through the downpour. Lightning flashed and the short intervals between light and sound, as well as the deafening crash of the thunder, made it plain that the great bolts were finding their way to the ground nearby. I knew we could be killed by lightning in such a storm. Perhaps that would be better than a showdown with Tiglon and his thugs.

Time and again as we ran, I searched my heart, wondering what empowered me to do what I was doing. Inexplicably, I was running pell-mell into the worst danger I had ever confronted.

Why? All I could think of at that moment was Jonah. Who was there on the entire earth he could count on to stand beside him in danger? He needed me. He was tragically alone and helpless.

And what about Shem? What drove him to stick with me, especially since he believed that what we were doing was foolish and dangerous?

And Rana! This was more heroism than I would ever have expected of her. She had been raised a hothouse flower. Where had this grit and determination to face danger come from?

It was pitch dark when we finally cleared the city walls. The lights of an occasional farm building blurred through the downpour. I was not even certain where we were going. I knew that Jonah had built himself a shelter of branches on a rise to the east of Nineveh. When he told me about it, I pictured a small hill I had often hiked to during student days, there to sit and gaze down on the great city stretched out below. I thought it must be the spot, but I couldn't be certain. If I was wrong about what I thought was the location of his hovel, there would be no way to locate him in this storm.

A moment later, in a flash of lightning, I saw the hill, off to the left. A muddy path led to the top, winding to the east side of the rise. If the hut were indeed on this hill facing the city, we would approach it from the rear, coming to the top through a grove of cedars. Perhaps the trees would provide us with some cover if we should need it. I had no plan of action, no idea what we would do if we should encounter Tiglon.

We stopped at the edge of the trees. Through the darkness, stark against the sky, I could see the hut. What a pitiful shelter! It had been constructed hurriedly, of branches, to keep the sun off Jonah's head as he sat waiting for wrath to fall on the city. Now, after weeks in sun and wind, the branches had mostly lost their dried leaves and the wind had caused the whole structure to fall into shambles. To think of such a hovel as shelter was ludicrous. Could Jonah possibly be inside?—lying dead under that pile of branches?

As if a hand had stopped it, the rain ceased. Leaving the cover of the cedars, we approached the hut, stopping to listen for any sounds that might penetrate the heavy air, warning us of danger. The black night was still and silent. Not even a breeze rustled the leaves.

At first, we could not find an entrance to this hovel of twisted, nearly leafless branches. The three of us finally squeezed inside at a place where the branches were not as closely intertwined.

"I hear someone breathing," whispered Rana breathlessly. She had not spoken a word since we had left the office.

It was impossible to see anything in the blackness. But Shem whispered, "I've stumbled over something—or someone. Come here."

Before I could speak, I almost fell over the body of a man lying on the floor. I felt around and found his face.

"Jonah, is it you?" I whispered. "Jonah, wake up. Wake up."

Shem had taken fire stones and tow from his wallet and was striking a flame. In a moment, he found an oil lamp and lighted it.

As the light shone in his face, Jonah stirred. I hardly recognized him. He had been beaten unconscious. Every inch of exposed skin was lacerated and bruised. One eye was swollen almost shut. The other was surrounded by hardened blood. "What is it? What do you want?" he muttered. I felt him carefully, gently. He groaned. I could find no broken bones, and couldn't guess whether he had sustained internal injuries.

"Is it you, Psychologist?" His voice grated dimly. "What are you doing here?"

"Jonah, what happened to you?"

"I don't know. Some men came from the city—I was leaving for—appointment—don't understand what they were angry about. They said—I had misled them—done them great harm. Then they beat me—must have passed out." Jonah shuddered in agony as he tried to turn his huge body toward me.

"You've been beaten nearly to death," I lamented. "Here is a bowl of water. Let me bathe and clean some of these cuts." I found some olive oil in a corner, and with it I cleaned Jonah's wounds. I bound up his cuts with pieces of cloth torn from my own garments. Then I covered him with my cloak.

"May I bathe his head with cool water?" Rana asked softly. I gave her the bowl of water and the wet compresses while I turned my attention to checking his pulse again. Meanwhile, Shem had found and lighted another lamp. "I'm going to look around outside," he said. I had forgotten that there might yet be danger.

Jonah had been silent for a long while. His eyes were closed. When Shem had squeezed outside, he opened his eyes, narrowed them, and asked me, "Why did you come? Why are you doing all this?"

"When you didn't arrive for your appointment," I replied, "I was worried about you. I had heard some rumors that made me concerned."

He seemed to be thinking about my reply.

Shem squeezed inside, and looked at Jonah. "They've gone, as far as I can see," he said. "I don't think they intended to kill you or they would have finished the job. They just wanted you to have a good taste of their anger."

As Shem spoke Jonah's eyes fell on Rana. By her dress, he must have known she was Assyrian. The trace of a smile flickered across his face. In response, she lightly stroked the prophet's forehead. "Anger?" Jonah asked weakly. "What anger? Why were they angry at me? I didn't even know them."

"There are some who believe they have fared ill from listening to your preaching, Jonah," I explained. "They blame you for losses their brief repentance cost them. Tonight, in the sultry heat, their anger erupted and they left their wine cups to come out and 'even the score'—as they see it."

"They won't be back," Shem said. "All they wanted was to make you taste pain— to 'pay' for the blunders they committed and blamed you for."

The prophet's eyes closed and I saw his features relax. Again, the suggestion of a smile played momentarily around the corners of his lips.

"Can you sleep, Prophet?" I asked, as Rana pulled the cloak over his shoulders.

"I feel very, very weary," he replied. "I think I can sleep. But first—I need to know—" he looked again at Rana—"why did you come? Why have you braved danger to help me, a Jew?"

Rana was caught off guard by his bluntness. Hesitating, she glanced at me, then stammered, "I—I'm not sure. No. I am sure. It's too much to explain, but—before tonight I never understood the meaning of love. Now I know it is not as I thought—not at all as I thought."

Jonah winced, whether from physical or inner pain, I did not know. "I have much more to learn than you, child," said the big man. His voice had grown soft, more gentle than I had ever heard it. His eyes closed, and his deep, regular breathing told us he had fallen asleep.

The next day, I sent a physician from the city to bind up Jonah's wounds properly. Rana insisted on going to him daily with food and drink. It was her tender nursing care which, Jonah later told me, eased the recovery of his body and taught him depths of compassion he had never before experienced.

Tiglon and two of his associates were convicted of assaulting the prophet and were soon serving time at hard labor.

Rana arranged an appointment with me on Jonah's behalf after a couple of weeks.

"Why did you come?" Jonah asked me when we had taken our old familiar places in my consulting room. "What was I to you? You could have been hurt or killed. Yet you cared enough to come to my hovel in that terrible storm, to bind up my wounds. And I have showed you nothing but anger. Why did you come?"

"I came," I answered, "because you were hurt and in danger. When I have been in need, Yahweh has come to me in love. I wanted to give some of that love to you."

"How different were the two visits I had that night," Jonah mused. "They were the only two visits anyone has paid to my hut. The one was a visitation of justice, to even the score. The other was a visit of mercy, to bind my wounds. I gave you blows you did not deserve. Nor, for that matter, had God done anything to deserve my blind fury. In return for my anger, both you and Yahweh brought me healing and mercy."

"So Yahweh came to you too," I reflected.

"Yahweh came. He entered my hut with you and your friends, for what the young woman discovered was Yahweh's love. She told me how His *giving* love had replaced the *taking* love she had always known. It was in Yahweh's love that you ministered to me. And it is even now His love that heals the sickness of my soul!"

"Your inner bruises are healing too, then?" I prompted.

"They are healing well, Psychologist!" he replied, and for the first time in the history of our relationship, he smiled at me without wrath! "How different it all appears! Yahweh has not only visited me in love, He's spoken to me in mercy. And since that night of storms, I see things that are new to me.

"I see myself as I am—or was. I came like the thugs: angry over injustice, certain I knew what justice was, though I did not. So blind was my hatred, I would willingly have assaulted Yahweh, as in their blind ignorance, the thugs assaulted me.

"To my twisted vision, God's mercy on Nineveh was as evil as my warning cry in the streets had been to my assailants—though that word I resented was God's own love, sparing their very lives!

"I did not understand God's love," he continued exuberantly, "and I thought it a weakness in Him until I saw His love embodied in you and your friends. You forgave me my stubbornness—and, unaccountably, you loved me.

"Yahweh, too, has revealed His love for me in spite of the wretched bitterness I heaped on Him. He has showed me that in His mercy He is *not* unjust, and that, one day, a day we do not yet see, justice and mercy will flow together to renew the earth."

"Has He forgiven you, Prophet?"

"He has, Psychologist."

"Have you forgiven Him?"

"Yes. Oh, yes," answered my former patient.